How to Make Your Own

# RECREATION

# and HOBBY

# ROOMS

# How to Make Your Own
# RECREATION
# and HOBBY
# ROOMS

## by Ralph Treves

POPULAR SCIENCE

HARPER & ROW
New York, Evanston, San Francisco, London

Library of Congress Catalog Card Number: 68-31229
ISBN: 0-06-014364-9

**First Edition, 1968**
 **Four Printings**

**Second Edition, Revised and Updated, 1976**

Tenth Printing, 1979

Manufactured in the United States of America

# CONTENTS

# ACKNOWLEDGMENTS

The author would like to thank the following companies for their cooperation in supplying photographs for this book:

ARMSTRONG CORK COMPANY

THE MASONITE COMPANY

MARLITE DIVISION, MASONITE COMPANY

WESTERN LUMBER MANUFACTURERS ASSOCIATION

UNITED STATES PLYWOOD CORPORATION

GOLD BOND—NATIONAL GYPSUM COMPANY

SHEETROCK—UNITED STATES GYPSUM COMPANY

LIBBY-OWENS-FORD

THE BILCO COMPANY

THE MAJESTIC COMPANY

EMERSON ELECTRIC COMPANY

PORTLAND CEMENT ASSOCIATION

PITTSBURGH CORNING CORPORATION

OWENS-CORNING COMPANY

GEORGIA-PACIFIC COMPANY

SLANT-FIN COMPANY

INTERNATIONAL OIL BURNER COMPANY

# CHAPTER ONE

# MORE LIVING SPACE

YOUR FAMILY is missing plenty if your home doesn't have a recreation room or den. The standard six-room house that once was so satisfactory suddenly seems cramped. It is no longer adequate for the busy go-go generation with its ever-widening horizon of interests, its increasing leisure, and its greater participation in sports, scholastic efforts, social activities, and hobbies.

Few expenditures pay off as handsomely as does the outlay for a family playroom. The addition expands your living space, providing a source of pleasure and comfort for every member of the family. And, unique among all the things you buy, it is likely that you will recoup all or most of the amount expended for the improvement in the increased value of your home.

Whatever you call it—a family room, rumpus room, recreation room, game room, club room, den—it's perfect for gathering around the TV, for listening to the hi-fi, for storing your collection of records, for screenings of photo slides and films, for a dart board, ping pong, or other games. If you go in for folk dancing, the smooth tile floor is perfect for sashaying. The room also will be used for your bridge games, for sewing sessions, and for informal entertaining.

It's the place where Dad can relax in a bulky recliner chair that wouldn't be allowed in the living room. When Mother has a bridge party, or hosts a committee meeting of her civic or church group, the casual den furniture can be shifted easily to accommodate all the guests. Sis can have her school crowd in for a dancing party without cutting up the rugs, while Junior has a place to set up his mineral collection or keep the gear of whatever his particular interest is at the moment.

The den also serves as a comfortable guest room on occasion. And that doesn't mean furnishing the place with massive old-time sleeper sofas that have to be opened for use as a bed. Foam rubber has changed all that; slim modern couches with foam padding require no setting-up exercises to get them ready. A pair of these couches, at right angles in a corner of the room, provides a conversational seating arrangement and takes up minimum space.

Perhaps what's most important to you would be a practical workshop equipped for cabinetmaking or general home maintenance chores. Or does your dream wish run to a complete gymnasium with parallel bars, punch bag, wrestling mat, exercise cycle, and even a separate shower or a sauna to relax workaday tensions?

If you're interested in photography, wouldn't it be great to have an efficient darkroom, all set up to use at any free time without lengthy preliminaries?

Whatever your sport or hobby, whether it's pottery making, billiards, tropical fish breeding, wood carving, model building, or collecting, it will be more enjoyable when you have a proper place and the facilities to pursue it.

Almost any home can be enlarged in some way, either internally or with an addition to the structure. With sensible planning, making the maximum use of your home possibilities, you could have both a workshop or hobby room and a serivceable recreation room, plus lots of additional storage space. How it can be done depends on the kind of house you have, its layout, the size and shape of your lot, and local building ordinances. And, of course, the cost.

Perhaps you have previously attempted such an expansion and were blocked by some particular difficulty, such as the location of the basement furnace, a staircase or window, or low attic clearance. It's time to take a second

Typical messy "storage" cellar is not only a fire hazard but also a sorry waste of space that can be made into an attractive recreation room for family use.

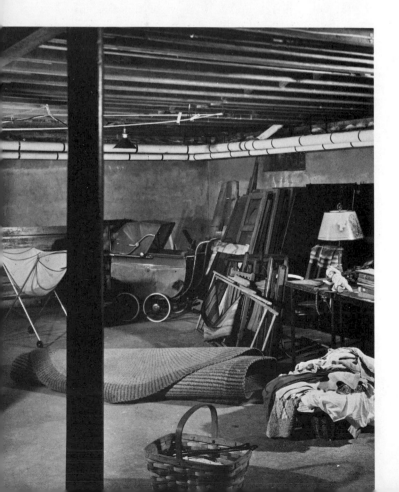

A well-arranged basement with wide stairway, an entry direct from the outside, and clear open space provides a ready-made situation for finishing into a practical room.

look. The suggestions given in the following chapters, based on extensive experience with home renovations and improvements, may present a completely new and satisfactory solution to a specific problem, enabling you to proceed. The marvelous new materials that have revolutionized construction techniques, and recent modifications of local building codes, may now make possible a home expansion project that once had been abandoned as hopeless.

If you have a basement, you're more than halfway home with the project even if it now seems a damp, cold, and dreary place. Improved floor coverings, prefinished wall panels and acoustical ceiling tiles, together with efficient zone heaters, dehumidifiers, exhaust fans and cooling systems, and clever lighting effects, can make the place truly attractive and livable.

An attic usually isn't suitable as a family recreation room, but with adequate noise insulation it can serve well for the younger set as a playroom, and it is just fine for hobbies such as oil painting and pottery making, or for a study room or home office.

Don't give up on this possibility just because the attic seems very small, has a low ceiling, or lacks a convenient stairway. But if for any reason you can't use the basement or attic, or you are determined to have a large den on the main floor of the house, the most practical low-cost expansion may be to convert a screened porch or attached garage. Adding a complete extension at one part of the house is, of course, more complex and certainly more expensive, but even in this case the project can be kept within bounds by astute planning and by doing part or all of the work yourself.

3

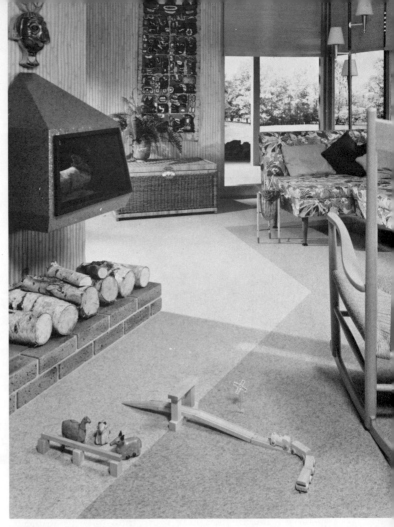

Beautifully designed family room from a converted garage has large floor-to-ceiling window walls, looking out on the open garden. Wall-mounted fireplace adds a hearty glow plus heat in winter weather.

**PROBLEMS OF HOME IMPROVEMENT.** When embarking on a major home improvement project, like finishing a basement or building a room onto the house, the homeowner often faces some difficulties. In some situations the difficulties are overwhelming, and it's a lot better to know about them before-hand, even if it means dropping the whole idea, than to go ahead and get in deeper than you had expected. When started on an improper footing, plenty of troubles can show up, causing either greater cost than anticipated, or dissatisfaction with the results because of some unforeseen fault. Examples might be finishing a basement that continues to be damp and musty-smelling, or building a room extension without adequate insulation so that it is uncomfortably chilly.

Another important question is whether a considerable investment in the project is economically sound. Common sense dictates that consideration be given to certain pertinent aspects, such as the neighborhood trend toward higher or lower prices, the length of time you expect to remain in the present house, and whether a substantial part of the improvement cost will be reflected in the resale price when you want to sell.

**Resale value.** Development homes that are all almost alike, built at the same time and sold at a uniform price, will very likely have a pegged resale value no matter how much you put in for improvements. But this is not a hard-and-fast rule; some neighborhoods are on the way up, so that any improvement you make will be adequately reflected when you go to sell.

You might keep in mind, too, that finishing the basement or attic is not likely to result in an increased tax assessment, but any exterior addition such as converting an open porch to an all-weather one will most surely bring a moderate tax increase.

**Switching houses.** A decision on whether to remodel or switch houses usually hinges on the degree to which the family is rooted in the community. Most families, because of neighborhood ties and other attachments, prefer to remain in their present homes amid familiar surroundings, even when they could afford the purchase of a larger house that contains the desired recreation room.

It's fun and games in this cleverly designed family room of luxurious size and decoration. Walls of rough-textured Masonite Style-Tex panels complement the massive ceiling beams.

Knotty pine in light pickled finish is still highly popular. Floor design in bright red and gray gives a festive air which is backed up by the friendly bar for pleasant entertaining at home.

There also is a reluctance to move because it would mean transferring the children to other schools, with all that involves such as missing their old playmates, adjusting to a new school curriculum, and even risking the loss of some scholastic credits.

It's not so easy, either, to sell one home and buy another. There's the task of finding a buyer for the present house, the time-consuming search for a new one, the uncertainties and worries in making the final choice, the red tape in arranging a new mortgage, the problems of coordinating the times for yielding possession of the old house and moving into the new one. And with it all, there's the prospect of giving up the house you have and know about, to acquire one in which you may be confronted with a whole new list of short-comings and problems.

**Hidden expenses.** The financial factors are not so clear cut either. Perhaps you could sell your present home for $25,000 and buy another that is some-what larger and has a good recreation room for $30,000. But the difference is much more than the obvious $5,000. The hidden costs could add another $2,000 to $4,000 and even more to the switch.

First there is the considerable brokerage cost for the sale. Then the new mortgage may have a higher interest rate than the one you now have, and in any event there are mortgage charges that may run to several hundred dol-lars for investigation, legal, and filing fees.

The buyer of your home may have his own financing arrangements, in which case you would have to pay off the entire old mortgage from the sale proceeds. But there's a hitch—the bank may require a pre-payment penalty and that could mean a substantial unexpected expense. Closing costs for the new house, plus attorneys' fees for both the sale and purchase, might add $500 or more. And then there are still the large bills for moving, redecorating, and all the incidentals. The figures given here are of course arbitrary and are intended only as a general illustration.

6

On with the dance! Easily moved furniture lets the floor be cleared for pleasant cocktail parties. Record player is conveniently placed behind the bar, with a graphic dance chart for the novice.

When all is considered, you'll most likely come to the conclusion that making the most of the home you now have, and are devoted to, will leave you far ahead in both cost savings and satisfaction.

**How much for a room?** Cost is certainly an important and often the deciding factor, and is taken into account in each of the suggested projects that follow, with emphasis on money-saving alternatives. Compromises often are necessary to keep the cost in line, and that may mean getting a bit less than you may have originally wanted—room size may be kept down, some interesting features dropped, or lower-cost materials substituted.

It's easy, when available funds are unlimited, to call in an architect, tell him to get you the "best," then shell out $4,000 to $10,000 for a single room addition. But when the project is carefully designed to take advantage of existing possibilities and other economies such as modular dimensioning and shell construction, the cost can be brought down to a reasonable level that makes the project easier to swing.

**Do-it-yourself role.** How much of the work you can do yourself will depend on the extent of your previous experience with various phases of the project, and the amount of leisure time you can devote to it. If you've had some experience with carpentry, very likely you can handle the wall framing, roof decking, ceiling furring, window installing, paneling, built-ins, and other important parts of the job.

Even if you have done little of this work before, there's much that you can safely tackle if you're willing to take the time and patiently follow instructions available from many good books and magazines.

7

Table tennis, anyone? Or chess? Or just a relaxed session listening to the latest tunes. Illustrations in the "windows" of this basement retreat are photo murals of charming outdoor scenes.

**Learning as you work.** Remember that doing the work is the best way to learn. Also, working with your hands is really relaxing and enjoyable. You'll soon develop the needed skills, and the work will go faster and better as you go along. Others can, so can you. What may have appeared to be a highly involved technique quickly becomes a casual and confident activity when you gain experience and capability. There's no better and more productive way to spend your vacation, or weekend leisure days, and it's great fun, too!

The details and techniques for doing most of the construction and finishing work—from footings and wall framing, to paneling and tile laying—are described in Chapter 12 at the end of this book so that you can conveniently refer to them as the occasion arises. An advantage of this arrangement is that you will know at a glance the scope and details of the specific work involved; this will enable you to decide which parts are in your baliwick, and which should be left to a pro.

Avoid pitfalls that will increase the cost or affect your satisfaction with the results. You want the project to improve, not damage your home, so plan carefully and avoid cutting too many corners. Make sure that the work conforms to established safety standards, zoning ordinances, and the building code requirements.

Observe the guidelines when contracting out any of the work—many a homeowner has found himself entangled in exasperating disputes, slapped with a lien by mechanics he didn't even know were on the job, and in a few cases lost his house because of liability suits.

This is not meant to discourage you. The checklist in Chapter 11 will help you keep things on an even keel. Most craftsmen you will deal with—carpenters, electricians, masons, tile setters, and others—are honest and straightforward people, highly skilled, eager to please. You will most likely find it a happy relationship, and will be glad to recommend them to neighbors, as others have to you.

# CHAPTER TWO

# SIZING UP YOUR HOUSE

HOUSES COME in any number of sizes, shapes, layouts, structural details, and age. Some are exceedingly compact, with hardly an inch leeway anywhere, others are perfectly square or ramble off in every direction and at a multitude of levels. So many homes are tightly squeezed onto their lots, others have ample land area for spreading out.

Whatever the type, space must be found, or added, to make a recreation room. A good first step in this project is to get a set of the original blueprints for your home, and a copy of the land survey. These will be important aids in planning any interior renovation or addition, and will be of great help in avoiding serious mistakes. A set of the original plans most likely can be borrowed from the architect or builder of your home, if you know who he is. A more dependable source is the local building department, which has a set of the plans on file and will make copies available to the homeowner for just a few dollars to cover the cost of search and making the copies.

These blueprints contain accurate interior dimensions, show the exact location of doors and windows, specify which walls are load-bearing and which are just partitions that can be knocked down without the need for reinforcing beams. Some home plans even include provisions for future additions. Study the plans carefully to see whether any of the walls that you intend to open up or demolish contain hidden steam pipes or water lines, as these may be difficult or costly to divert.

**WHAT WILL IT COST?** No need to wait until you've definitely decided on the specific finishing or construction details that will be done, and have drawn up or obtained fairly complete plans, to get approximate costs for the project. There are considerable price differences in individual situations and localities, the choice and quantity of materials, and whether the work will be done entirely or only in part by a contractor.

You can arrive at a workable estimate by making up lists of materials, computing the total cost for varying grades and qualities from prices supplied by your local dealers, then adding liberal guesses based on the experiences of friends and neighbors of what you would have to pay for those phases of the work that will be done by professionals, such as the masonry foundation, framing, brickwork or siding, electrical and heating installations, plumbing, floor tiles, roofing and others.

Some approximate cost ranges are given here to serve as a starting point for your computations. If your figures differ widely, or estimates from contractors are far off the mark, then some modifications of the plans may be necessary, if you want to stay within these limits. Building materials have held to fairly close prices for many years, only lumber showing any extensive increase. Materials generally account for a fourth to a third of the total outlay, the rest covering labor, fees, insurance, subcontractors and other charges. Professional services like those of electricians, plumbers, and carpenters have gone up considerably, and here is where you can score substantial savings with your own efforts.

| | |
|---|---|
| BASEMENT FINISHING | Materials, about $500 to $1,200, a complete job between $2,000 and $4,000. Add $900 to $2,500 for an extra powder room. |
| ATTIC ROOM | $600 to $1,200 for materials; $3,000 to $5,000 for job done by contractor. If roof dormers are needed, cost may be $1,200 to $3,000 more. |
| CONVERTING GARAGE OR PORCH | $900 to $1,500 for materials, complete job by contractor will run $3,000 to $5,000 without foundation. |
| NEW ADDITION TO HOUSE | Figure from $18 to $36 per square foot for the bare room, depending on type of foundation and whether walls are brick or frame. A room 12-by-15 feet will cost $3,200 to $6,480 for frame construction, $3,000 and more for a high foundation and brick walls. |
| FIREPLACE | A masonry fireplace would add $2,000 to $4,000 to the cost, but you can have a complete metal prefabricated unit for as little as $350, installing it yourself. |

**UPLIFTING THE BASEMENT.** By any standard you could apply, the basement offers the best deal in a recreation room, giving you the largest possible room space with lots of fine extras, and for the very least cost.

The reason is obvious. Everything is right there—the walls, floor, ceiling, even the heat and electricity. All it takes is some finishing to make it more comfortable and more attractive. And you can do as little or as much of this as you wish, a little at a time as the budget permits, or all at once to get the maximum advantage for your family's immediate use.

Just put down $100 worth of asphalt tile on the floor, and presto! The drab cement floor is sealed against its dust and moisture; in its place is a clean, smooth, colorful play area that can serve many purposes.

Go a bit further to cover the foundation walls and ceiling with inexpensive materials, put in additional lighting, and there's a real room that is presentable and livable, as useful as any in the house. If you compounded the investment by selecting such materials as fine prefinished Weldwood plywood of popular hardwoods, or sleek Marlite plastic-coated panels in the most attractive wood and novelty patterns, your room will also gain character and a luxurious appearance.

**Cost ranges.** Here are the approximate costs for materials for a 16-by-20-foot room, if you do the installation yourself:

| | |
|---|---:|
| 320 square feet of asphalt floor tile and adhesive | $120.00 |
| 18 panels of 4-by-8-foot Sheetrock gypsum board | 54.00 |
| Acoustical ceiling tiles | 50.00 |
| Moulding trim | 38.00 |
| Furring strips, 1-by-2 inch | 40.00 |
| 2-by-4s for framing | 38.00 |
| Four fluorescent light strips, and wiring supplies | 80.00 |
| Nails, floor cement, taping compound | 30.00 |
| Total | $450.00 |

If you want to spend somewhat more, here's another example:

| | |
|---|---:|
| Prefinished ¼-inch real plywood wall panels | $210.00 |
| Vinyl asbestos floor tiles | 120.00 |
| Textured ceiling tiles | 100.00 |
| 2-by-4 wall and partition framing | 100.00 |
| Furring for ceiling tiles | 25.00 |
| Wall trim | 65.00 |
| Recessed fluorescent fixtures and wiring cable | 135.00 |
| Nails, floor adhesive, corrugated metal for boxing water pipes, etc. | 45.00 |
| Total | $800.00 |

How else could you obtain a pleasant 320-square-foot room for $450 to $800? But just because the improvement can cost so little, that's all the more reason to spend as much extra as you think worth while to make the room look even better, more inviting, and more practical to serve your needs and become a really interesting entertainment center in your home. Let yourself go! Add a built-in bar to serve your guests in style. Set up a hi-fi record player for your musical pleasure. Lend decorative touches for style and beauty.

Basement rooms offer several distinct advantages. They are removed from the usual traffic areas of the house, provide more privacy, and allow greater leeway in noise-making because of the natural acoustical values.

It must be acknowledged that many people retain old-time prejudices against the basement as living quarters, dating back to the days when cellars were tainted with coal bins, cobwebs and mildew. The area seemed dank and forbidding, a sort of nether region shut off from the rest of the house, often having an entrance only from the outside. Cellars were too hot and damp in summer bonechilling cold in winter. Obstructions like low water pipes or heating ducts often were right at the entranceway, while a poorly located furnace took up an excessive amount of space, leaving only small open areas

Even basement rooms that were finished some years ago lacked appeal. Lighting was very poor, wood flooring soon became warped and springy, knotty pine walls darkened to a dreary brown. Narrow and shaky staircases weren't very inviting.

If you now have a finished basement room but have not been using it much because it's dim and uninviting, it's time to take a second look. Maybe some deficiency that detracts from its appearance or effectiveness can be easily corrected. Present day materials and ideas provide practical answers to most of these shortcomings.

A basement room can indeed be as pleasant as any in the home when it is bright and warm, dry, attractively set up, and easily maintained. Well-designed wall cabinets and storage closets encourage putting away all items not in use, so that the recreation room always is neat and tidy.

**Concrete sealer.** The most important single contribution toward uplifting the cellar to livable status was the development of asphalt tiles. These were the first that could be laid directly on the cement floor below grade, simultaneously sealing the cellar against floor dampness and the alkali of the concrete, and providing a colorful, smooth, easy to-clean surface.

Now the venerable asphalt tile has been superseded by the more stable vinyl-asbestos tiles. These are available in all the light colors and in many interesting patterns with all the beauty of marble terrazo or mosaic tiles. One of the new sheet floorings, Armstrong's Corlon cushioned vinyl sheeting with a backing that is impermeable to alkali from the concrete, is a decided advance in flooring for basements and all other floors.

Floor covering should be selected in the lightest shades to help brighten the room. Asphalt tile originally was much more expensive in the light colors than the blacks and browns. Now, however, there is no appreciable price differential for light colors in the vinyl asbestos tiles, which come in white, bright yellow, and similar attractive shades. A floor sealed with the tiles also can have carpeting, which does so much to make the room pleasant and comfortably warm.

With the addition of light-colored wall paneling, practical built-ins, plenty of fluorescent light fixtures and lamps, and perhaps a colorful wall mural of a photographed outdoor scene, the basement rec room will be a favorite for everyone from the kiddies to grandparents, in good weather and foul, summer and winter.

**Include hobby rooms.** Once you get started on the plans, you'll find it possible to arrange the valuable basement space to provide a workshop, study, or office. The accessibility of the water lines and the electric circuit box makes it easy to set up a laundry room, with washer, dryer, and tubs. The laundry can do double duty as a darkroom, requiring only a counter and the means for lightproofing the windows.

An extra toilet, with shower stall, will be a great convenience, especially if the family room is used occasionally for putting up overnight visitors, or there is a separate guest room. The gym can be incorporated as part of the recreation room, or arranged in separate quarters if there's enough space.

**USING THE ATTIC.** Whether you can use the attic for a hobby or play-room will depend on several circumstances, such as overhead clearance, access to the upper regions, etc., as described in Chapter 5. Heating, ventilation and cooling are easily provided. Other problems, however, may represent a real barrier.

If you decide that the attic offers the best possible additional space, it may be worth while to provide dormers, or to raise one entire side of the roof to enlarge the space with greater head clearance.

In two-story houses, with the bedrooms on the second floor, the attic may have limited use as a recreation room. It would be fine for a study or music room, for a ping pong table and other games. Noise may be a deterrent, but this can be minimized by the liberal use of floor insulation.

**CONVERTING THE PORCH.** If building an extension onto the house seems the only alternative, then an attached rear porch might be the nucleus for this project. The porch can be enclosed and winterized, heat and light installed, the floor leveled flush with the house floors. In such a porch den, large sliding glass doors for access to the rear yard provide the greatest amount of light and an unobstructed view. Much of the other windows of the porch room would have to be closed off to improve the heating. An air conditioner and an adequate space heater in this room will make it comfortable for year-round use, and an open fireplace can lend a touch of ultimate luxury.

**COMBINATION ROOMS.** When you just don't have space for a separate party room, and building an addition onto the house isn't feasible, the only practical solution is to double up on a room so that it serves different purposes. The present laundry room may be of greater size than needed, or it can be en-larged by incorporating with it an adjacent hallway, entrance hall, or backyard porch, by removing a partition wall. In another example, limited basement space is extended by including the laundry within the recreation room rather than occupying a separate area.

The laundry appliances, hamper, and tub are concentrated along one wall, taking up a depth of less than 3 feet. Shelves and cabinets above the appliances hold the detergents, bleaches and other necessary supplies within easy reach.

A row of double-fold louver doors or an accordion-type folding door closes off the laundry space, leaving the rest of the room in the clear for the family. But the laundry itself is never cramped—just swing the doors open and there's the whole room in which to move about.

If cutting table, sewing machine, and ironing board are needed for the laundry, these items of equipment may be incorporated into the room plan in such a way that they are folded into the wall, or rolled out from under a coun-ter when needed.

**CONVERT THE GARAGE.** One effective means of achieving a large recrea-tion room at moderate cost is to incorporate an attached or adjacent garage. This project will depend on several factors, enumerated later, but it provides an exceptionally large space. If the garage is separated from the house by a breezeway, this can be fully enclosed for a weather-protected passage. A converted garage will blend right into the rest of the house, after the overhead garage doors are removed and the opening finished with siding or brick facing to match.

There are other alternatives if these are lacking. Building a complete extension to obtain a recreation room is quite expensive, but the cost can be kept down considerably by doing a large part of the work yourself, particularly inside finishing.

An extension should take advantage of any features of the house: for instance, if there is a projection of any length at one part of the rear, the room can be planned so that both the rear wall of the house and the side wall of the projection are utilized, thus minimizing the extent of the construction work.

**HOUSE EXTENSION.** One basic consideration is the problem of "tying in" the new structure to the old. If the house is of wood or aluminum siding, it would be necessary to remove some section of the old siding, and erect the wood frame so it is integral with the original walls. In a brick house, all brick courses should be aligned with those of the original walls, and the half brick at the corners removed so that the new courses are jointed in.

In the new construction, which is discussed in fuller detail in Chapter 7, the main questions to be decided will be the type of foundation and floor; whether to have a curtain foundation and a crawl space, or merely build the new room on a slab if the house floor level is close to grade.

Heating may be obtained from the present furnace, whether it is hot water, steam, or hot air, if the system is able to carry the additional demand, or by installing a separate space heater, fueled by electric, gas or oil, and supplemented by a prefabricated fireplace to burn wood or coal.

**Cantilevered extension.** One other possibility is that of a cantilevered enlargement of a room to make it adequate for a den. That is a system of supporting the extension on projecting beams attached to the present floor joists of the house, but is practical only for an extension of just a few feet. For larger construction above grade level, the new floor is supported on lally columns with open space below. This type of room may extend out about as far as desired, even 20 feet or more.

**Modular dimensions.** Important cost savings are achieved when construction and remodeling plans are based on the modular increments of the materials to be used. For example, standard brick and concrete block can be used in their full size, without cutting and fitting, when the wall is an even 8 feet long, while one that is half a foot shorter will require considerable extra labor and a waste of material. The basic modular unit is 4 feet. Concrete blocks are standard 15¾ inches long, which together with the mortar joint lays in at 16 inches. Thus, three blocks will equal a course covering 4 feet. Plywood panels are a standard 4-by-8-foot size, are quickly installed without cutting, over studs which are spaced 16 inches apart on centers. Thus a room addition 12-

by-16 feet in size can be erected and finished at a lower cost than a smaller room of 11-by-15 because there are less waste of materials and labor time.

**Plans available.** Modular dimensions are featured in plans for two basic room extensions which were printed in the April 1967 issue of *Popular Science*. The rooms are as follows: One room is square, 16-by-16; the other oblong 12-by-20. They are designed for additions to any type of house, constructed in the most proficient manner using standard materials without waste.

The simple basic style may be applied to the front, side or rear of a house, the oblong shape joining the house on either the wider or shorter side. The plans are adapted to three roof designs: flat, shed, and gabled, to conform to most house styles.

The design has been worked out particularly with the do-it-yourselfer in mind, and the article contains all the required construction details. For $5 you can get a complete blueprint signed by a registered architect, suitable for filing with the local building department and to obtain builders' estimates. The blueprint is available from Popular Science, 355 Lexington Avenue, New York, N.Y. 10017.

**DO-IT-YOURSELF GUIDE.** This book is intended to guide you in planning and designing recreation and hobby rooms, to caution you about the pitfalls, and help get the project off the ground.

It doesn't attempt to provide all the precise "how to" details on doing the work, as this would involve extensive technical data for many phases of the project—wall framing, foundations, roofing, siding, floor laying and tiling, wall paneling, heating, electrical installation, and many other subjects—which could not be presented in a single book, unless superficially.

However, a chapter is devoted to outlining the basic techniques of the work involved, so that you can estimate the extent of the work, and schedule the sequence of each phase of the project. In some instances, data is given in sufficient detail to direct you in doing the work yourself.

# CHAPTER THREE

# THERE'S FUN IN DECORATING

A FAMILY room is where the action is. When you're going to all the trouble and expense of adding a room, certainly you'll want to make it as practical, cheerful, and interesting as possible. Keep the decorative style in a lighthearted and informal spirit so that the room will lend itself to casual enjoyment and yet present an engaging appearance. Let your creative talents take wing and make it as glamorous as a nightclub, as sparkling as an ice cream parlor, as gay as a circus.

The decorating aspect is concerned with every part of the remodeling and finishing project, from the basic layout to the design of built-ins and selection of colors and accessories. Each detail has a role in determining the ultimate success of the recreation room, whether it becomes a focal point of the family's leisure living, or a forgotten hideaway.

**PLANNING AHEAD.** There are two ways to go about the task of decorating. One is to wait until the room is completed, then study its shape and features in an effort to achieve the best results with what you have. Another, more practical and economical method, is to visualize the finished room beforehand and integrate the decorative scheme into the basic plans so that construction details, layout, and materials harmonize and enhance the ultimate concept.

An example is the use of a dramatic centerpiece for the dominant note, such as a large photo mural in full color or a poster. Particularly effective is a mounted swordfish that was your own proud catch. You may decide that the display would be more impressive when recessed into a niche rather than on the wall surface. It's obviously easier to provide a recess of the required dimensions while putting up the wall studs than to cut into the wall paneling after it is fully installed. So work with a floor plan to design your room right from the start.

Keep in mind, too, the main activities that will be pursued. Will the room be mostly for relaxing and enjoying music recordings? Then you can plan for comfortable chair groupings at the center of the room, with bookcases and audio cabinets occupying most of the walls. Will the room be used by children for free-wheeling play and games? Then keep the floor area as open as possible,

16

Discotheque party room has gay and amusing colors throughout. Bold stripes on walls are continued in the floor ti!e design. A built-in bar at one end, record cabinet and audio unit at the other part of the wall, leave the floor area clear for dancing. The platform at center is on casters. Note the turned stairway entrance.

and provide plenty of easily reached storage places for keeping toys and playthings out of the way when not in use. For the family mineralogist, you could have illuminated display cases around the walls. And even dramatics can be encouraged with a stage setting, draw curtains and all.

Games may be part of your plans, so include them in. A shuffleboard deck can be included in the floor tile design. Darts are simple enough—just a target on the wall but in a protected location. Ping pong, even billiards can be arranged with storage places for disassembled tables when they are not in use. For the golfer, there's a year-round putting green to keep his stroke in practice. A checkerboard or chess table will give everyone many hours of pleasure.

Do you entertain frequently with socials or cocktail parties, or go in for folk dancing sessions? Then the room shape should be kept as square as possible, wall cabinets arranged so they do not project deeply into the room, and furniture selected of the type that can be folded up and stored out of the way. Long benches built along the wall can take the place of chairs. Parties for duplicate bridge sometimes require four or more bridge tables. Include in the primary plans storage facilities for these tables and chairs so the room can readily be cleared for other uses.

While you're at it, develop a decorative theme for the room to reflect your own special interests and hobbies. In each of the activities listed above, an expressive note will highlight the events or purposes.

Another well-planned basement room for children's use has attractive snack counter and toy display racks. Exercise bar is seen along the left wall with illuminated aquarium behind it.

A gay atmosphere will be accented for the cocktail party crowd with intriguing accents of cutouts in the shape of high hats and dancing slippers, long-stemmed glasses and musical grace notes and pictures of neon-lighted nightclub entrances pasted to the walls. Your bridge-playing guests will appreciate decorative symbols of the game, in the shape of playing cards and a photo blowup of sensational scores. Folk dancers will appreciate photo murals of peasant dancers on the village green, in traditional native costumes, a fiddler and caller in full swing.

Are you a ski enthusiast? Extend the season of your sport all the year round by designing your recreation room in the style of a ski lodge! Are you intrigued with Oriental furnishings? Indulge your interest with distinctive Far East shoji screens, red lacquered chests, a laughing Buddha and bamboo furniture. Sailing buffs can make their landlocked deck exciting with the toss of a halyard, some pennants, and an anchor or two.

Give your imagination full rein and develop your own motif, whether it's Victorian or contemporary, Spanish, French Provincial, or South Seas style. It's your room and anything goes, from a safari hut to a Gay Nineties Cafe.

**SUGGESTED THEMES.** When a primary decorative theme has been chosen, your imagination will be stimulated to plan an appropriate design, and perhaps even inspire research into the subject. Many items can be purchased or obtained free that will carry the motif, or you well may be able to create some intriguing symbols of your own. These need not be expensive; many simple everyday articles can be adapted for the special purpose, or you may have them on hand as regular accessories for your sport or hobby.

For a tropical South Seas room, bind some palm fronds atop lally columns and wrap the poles with coarse palm matting. Tack colorful woven blankets and a sombrero onto the walls of a Mexican room. For the Spanish decor, hang a guitar, castanets, and shawls. If you're a wild game buff, plan an African safari room with jungle murals of a clutch of lions or herd of wildebeests, spread a zebra skin on the floor, add a set of native drums and a collection of carved wood face masks or other figures. A "hippie" room makes the mark with weird wall posters and strings of beads, overlaid with incense. For the angler, a fishing rod, lures, and landing net will do the trick, while the ski enthusiast can schuss right into his home ski lodge, particularly if it has walls of simulated half-logs and a massive fireplace.

Lightweight rattan furniture sets the decorative tone for this unique family room. Immense hood provides draft for the open log fireplace.

Here are some suggestions for room motifs, one of which may just hit the right note with you:

Oriental—Japanese
South Seas—Polynesian, South Pacific, Hawaiian
Mediterranean—Italian, Spanish, Moroccan
Contemporary—modern Scandinavian
Early American or Colonial
Victorian
Tennis
Ski lodge
Fishing
Scuba diving (underseas photo)
African room
Tropical
Mexican hacienda
Indian
English pub
Knotty pine
Paddock—horses
Aviator (gliding, soaring)
Calypso—Jamaican
Israeli
Gay Nineties
Theater
Music
French bistro, Parisian cafe
Ice cream parlor
Discotheque
Floridian
Sailing
Surfboarding
Circus, zoo
Wild West—cowboy
Hunting
Nursery—Mother Goose
Golfing
Photographic (family photos)

**LIGHTING THE NEW ROOM.** Good lighting cannot be stressed too strongly. That means illumination both for effect and for beauty. Do not depend on a single type of lamp such as fluorescent strips, but rather have a range of light sources that can be used separately or in combination. Clever lighting makes a room look larger and emphasizes its most attractive features. Include enough light switches in gangs of two or four at convenient locations, to give you selective light control for different occasions.

Well-lighted basement room is featured by large open space at center. Built-in serving counter is decorated with immense balusters. Old-time player piano is painted in gay colors for festive look.

For general illumination, strips of 40-watt fluorescent lamps give the greatest amount of light at lowest service cost. This is particularly important in a basement room where maximum and continuous lighting is essential. Remember that the basement gets very little daylight, so the lamps will be kept on all the time the room is used.

Four double 40-watt strips are a minimum to provide the light needed for a room 12-by-16 feet in size. These lamps may be arranged in single exposed strips on the ceiling, hidden back of wall cornices, or by recessing 2-lamp fixtures into the ceiling. If the fixtures have etched glass covering, or there are egg-crate light diffusers, some of the light is lost and should be supplemented by additional light sources.

**Lighted stairway.** The basement stairway has critical lighting requirements. At least one light at the very top, and two hooded floodlights along the steps, will make the stairway inviting and help avoid accidental falls. Two fluorescent strips, one on each side of the stairway, will make the area really bright all along the way. Three-way light switches at the stairway are almost mandatory.

Another effective light source is the high-hat type which consists of circular metal shells recessed flush into the ceiling tiles with a ringed diffuser at the opening. Bullet-shaped lamps with floodlight or spot bulbs can be located on the side walls or on poles, the light beam aimed at a wall mural or other decorative accent piece. These can be adjusted for bridge games when needed. For a more homey atmosphere, have a few table lamps around the room.

21

**CHOOSING MATERIALS.** When selecting the materials for your room, give sufficient consideration to the matter of easy maintenance. Choose materials that are easy to clean, and rugged enough to keep their new look for many years even under considerable use.

Basic ingredients of your room decoration are the floor tiles and wall panels, which are complemented by the furnishings and accessories.

For basements and other floors, Armstrong's Excelon vinyl-asbestos tile is resilient, exceptionally durable, unharmed by cleaners and grease, stays fresh and bright with just an occasional damp mopping. Vinyl Corlon tile, and Armstrong's hydracord-backed Corlon, are luxury floor coverings for any part of the house, including basement below-grade floors, and provide the widest range of exciting colors and patterns. Asphalt tile is now almost as expensive as vinyl asbestos, but ranks poor in soil resistance, has a tendency to become pitted from the weight of chair legs. All floor tiles can be installed by the do-it-yourselfer according to the instructions in Chapter 12, but sheet

The decorative theme here is that of the Mexican hacienda, as seen in the paneled doors, beamed ceiling, bricked archway. Interesting candleholders lend further accent.

A nautical theme is expressed in the accessories, including a canvas sea bag, lantern, and simulated wheel deck. The floor design includes an anchor, and the chairs of course are those usually found at the captain's table.

goods should be put down by a craftsman who has the experience to match the tightly butted seams.

Floor coverings now are available in exceptionally attractive designs and colors. Of particular note are the marble and terrazo patterns, and the flagstone arrangements. Other very interesting floor designs are mosaic, brick and quarry tile arrangements. A more complete listing is given in the chapter on materials.

Wall panels of prefinished plywood or plastic-coated hardboard provide the ingredient for uniquely beautiful and dramatic rooms. Marlite panels offer perhaps the widest assortment of handsome colors and patterns in natural wood grains, textured specialty surfaces that have the character of fine leather and tapestry textiles, and also decorator finishes in mosaics, embossed tiles, and many solid colors. Marlite panels are mirror-smooth, highly durable, and rugged enough to resist denting. These panels are particularly suitable for basement finishing, even where there may be some residual moisture.

Marlite also offers a number of attractive murals, in 5-by-5-foot and larger sizes. The pictorial scenes, in metallic gold and black on white backgrounds, can serve to establish your selected decorative motif for a South Pacific, Florentine, nautical and Oriental room.

**POSTERS TELL THE STORY.** An excellent aid for decorating your room are large posters of native scenes. You can get many of these from airlines, steamship companies, and travel bureaus of the different countries, showing skiers and bobsleds in Switzerland, architecture of Sweden, Old English pubs,

Not every family room can be as spacious as this one, but there's every reason to fit in a window greenhouse, and a large built-in aquarium. Staircase opens directly into the room.

Colorful zebra pattern decorates the bar and stools in this African room for intimate home entertaining.

Another attractive bar is decorated with series of half-round strips glued to the curved plywood facing. Note air conditioner that replaced a small basement window.

Simulated ceiling beams may be included in your design by forming boxed sections of hardwood plywood. The acoustical ceiling by Armstrong helps to quiet the sounds that are reflected around the room by wall surfaces.

and Mexican scenes. Pop art and fun posters are now sold at book stores and novelty shops.

One of the greatest contributions to an attractive and carefree family room is Formica plastic laminate for furniture and all exposed surfaces. Not only is the material almost indestructible and easy to clean with the wipe of a damp cloth, but it can be obtained in surfaces that match the color and graining of real wood and marble. A major advantage in the use of Formica is that it completely ends the need for finishing the wood of built-ins.

**BUILT-INS SET THE TONE.** Don't overlook the role of built-in furniture in creating the cozy atmosphere of your entertainment room. One of the most popular is a knotty pine bar, replete with rows of polished stemware and an array of fine liquors in their many colors and oddly shaped bottles. Some people equip their home bars with every provision for cordial entertaining, including high chairs, a stainless steel sink under the counter, a miniature refrigerator, and an electric ice shaver.

Floor-to-ceiling wall cabinets might contain bric-a-brac, books, a tropical fish aquarium, a built-in record player, and a television set. An important detail for music lovers is the installation of audio speakers, often recessed into the ceiling or at other suitable locations.

The party hostess will appreciate a convenient serving buffet, containing a sink and shelves for needed dishes and supplies, and a bank of electric outlets for toaster, percolator, and broiling grill to rustle up snacks for guests without the need for many trips to the kitchen. This pantry can be concealed behind folding louver doors to contribute to the room's appearance.

CHAPTER FOUR

# FINISHING A BASEMENT ROOM

THE PRIMARY stages in basement finishing involve framing the walls and putting up wall panels, covering the ceiling joists with acoustical tiles, laying floor tiles, boxing in pipes and columns, roughing in electric wires and connecting lights and receptacles, and completing the decorative details such as window enclosures, moulding trim, and heater openings.

Your first consideration is whether the basement is suitable for finishing into serviceable rooms. A basement is satisfactory for the purpose if it has adequate headroom—at least 7 feet 6 inches high—and is not subject to periodic flooding from the outside. In some cases, but not all, even these extreme deficiencies can be overcome. The causes of dampness and musty odors should be investigated, and it is certainly worth taking the trouble to eliminate such conditions.

Most dampness is due to condensation of vapor on the foundation walls and floor, which are in contact with the earth outside and are therefore colder than the atmosphere inside the house. Floor tiles and wall paneling go a long way to reduce or eliminate dampness by sealing the concrete and slowing condensation.

If the condition is due to minor seepage through porous walls or cracks, a treatment with hydrostatic mortar and pore-filling masonry paint usually works as a corrective measure. Proper drainage away from the house foundation of rain water from the roof downspouts often completely solves the problem of damp basements.

Exhaust fans will move concentrations of humid air, while a dehumidifier will be very helpful, taking gallons of water out of the air each day. Adding below-grade windows or enlarging the present windows, with adequate window well enclosures, may be necessary in some cases. The openings are made in a poured concrete foundation with a compressed air hammer. This is done very quickly by a contractor at a moderate cost, and will be useful also in providing more daylight in the basement.

**Wall joint sealer.** A common condition found in damp basements is seepage at the wall joint along the foundation footings. It is possible to seal the joints by widening them sufficiently to pack in a quick-setting joint cement and

A swinging room for teen gatherings makes the basement one of the most valuable areas of the home. Attractive and practical decorative features include the Armstrong Corlon floor with its circular figure, the mock stone fireplace with electric flame, and the draw draperies which appear to cover large windows.

an asphalt sealer. Here, too, the work should be done by a waterproofing expert. In some extreme cases, the only dependable correction is to put in a second foundation wall of poured concrete all around the inside after sealing the original wall with asphalt coating.

Low-level flooding usually can be controlled by banking earth against the foundation wall or building a barrier of concrete blocks to the necessary height all around the house. Where water entry is due to backing up of storm sewer water, a check valve in the sewer line usually is successful in controlling the back flow.

A chronic condition of heavy flooding can be solved only by community action involving the installation of adequate storm sewers and storage areas.

**Sump pump.** Where persistent water seepage through the floor is encountered from an underground spring or low water table, the solution may well

Comfortable family room in basement is spacious and uniquely decorated with carved spindle balusters plus hand railing at stairs, and long serving counter at rear. Note the fluorescent lamp on ceiling extending the full length of the staircase.

Archery hobbyists can indulge their sport safely in long basement playroom with guarded entrance. Pegboard wall holds the sportsman's supplies which also provide decorative accent.

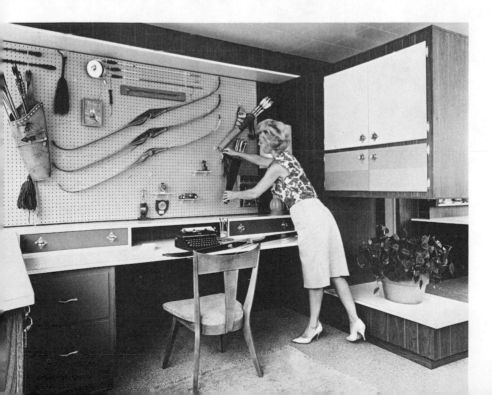

Cabinets in basement utilize excess space for specialized storage purposes such as the complete ski and golf outfits. All supplies are kept together, in and out of season, thus ending the mad last-minute hunt for missing items.

Well-equipped home workshop is compactly stored under the basement stairs when not in use, so the room can be used by the family. The saw and drawer cabinets are on casters for easy rolling.

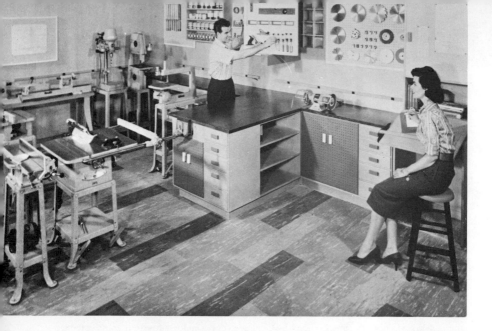

Nothing like a fully equipped workshop in your basement, permitting you to tackle all sorts of interesting projects. Tools in center of room are on casters so they can be turned to the direction needed by the work, or rolled out of the way for any other reason.

A splendid idea is this artistic rock garden arrangement at foot of basement stairs. The unit is faced with Masonite Marbletone, a hardboard with marble finish, which also covers the back wall.

The average basement is spacious, well-lighted, has ample ventilation for finishing into a recreation room. Problems regarding staircase and furnace location usually can be overcome. Low ceilings, dampness, obstructions by columns, and similar situations may complicate the basement project but in most cases can be solved at moderate cost.

Walls are framed out with studding for partitions and the finishing panels. Here the floor was finished with tile before the room project was started. Partition shown will separate the laundry and utility space from the recreation room.

Stud framing boxes in windows for decorative finishing later. Electric receptacle boxes are attached to the studs, as seen. Note that electric cable is carried between ceiling joists.

A recently developed method of framing out the walls with furring strips uses a bead of adhesive directly on the foundation wall. The furring is held with the contact adhesive, then the finish panel of Masonite Royalcote is glued in the same manner to the furring. But make sure that the furring strips are plumb and uniform, rather than merely following the contours of the wall.

Floor tiles are easily installed by a new method in which the adhesive is spread with a brush, just like paint, and the tiles simply placed in the ordered pattern arrangement. Floor may be finished so the room can be used before the wall paneling goes up.

Ceiling acoustical tiles are stapled to furring strips which are nailed across the joists. Once the furring is in place, the tiles go up very quickly. No insulation is needed in the ceiling of a basement room.

be the installation of a sump pit excavated in the basement floor, with a pump of adequate capacity to remove the water by pumping it into the sewer line or into the street. The sump has an automatic control switch, actuated by a float lever or diaphram. When the water reaches a predetermined level, the pump goes into action, and shuts off again, as the water level in the sump drops.

Extreme caution is essential when using any portable evacuation pump to clear out flooded water, as there is considerable danger of electric shock.

**Basement stairs.** In many homes, the stairway is in a difficult position, making access inconvenient, or the stairs are of such poor quality that they must be used with excessive care. Some stairs are little more than ladders, with shaky treads held merely by nails into the side stringers.

The right thing to do, in any event, is to replace the stairway with a sturdy new one having treads wedged into mortises, and with risers at the back of the treads. You can get stairs that are custom-made by millwork concerns to the specified dimensions—width of opening and ceiling height—and they do the rest, delivering the assembled stairway ready for installation. The only problem is how to get it inside the house and into position. In many locations, stringers and treads have to be reassembled at the site.

But if you're ordering new stairs, it may be well to consider whether a basic change in the stair position would be an improvement for a more attractive environment. If the stairs end up flush against an end wall, with barely any space to turn at the bottom, or if there is an obstruction such as a heating duct

Example of window treatment for the basement. The enclosure is trimmed with contoured molding. Door-type windows have gauze curtains.

or ceiling beam, you might be able to do better by rearranging the stairs with a platform halfway down, and a turn in direction to avoid the low ceiling, or to end the stairs facing directly into the main playroom.

Many people, particularly women, are jittery when walking on shaky or fragile stairs. It is important that the treads be of sufficiently thick stock to feel solid underfoot, the stringers securely fastened or supported, and the treads firmly wedged.

**Dowel stairs.** A good design for basement stairways uses 2-inch diameter clothespole dowels, set vertically at each of the stair treads, to serve for hand grips in place of a railing. This gives the stairway an open look that is always attractive and particularly useful because it overcomes the enclosed nature of the downstairs area.

A useful additional detail is to set the vertical dowels so that they can be easily removed when you need extra clearance to carry large items like laundry appliances or plywood panels into the basement. The dowel ends are fitted with smaller dowel pins that slip into holes drilled in the bottom plate, which is attached along the stair stringer.

The top ends of the dowels go into holes that are drilled completely through the plate that is nailed to the ceiling joist along the stair opening. Thus, when any dowels are to be removed, simply lift them so that the pin clears the hole in the bottom plate, then slip the end out of the top plate.

When in normal position, the dowels are quite secure and cannot fall out, because any weight put on them by a person on the stairway only bears down on the dowel base. The dowels can come out only when they are lifted sufficiently so the pins clear the recess in the bottom.

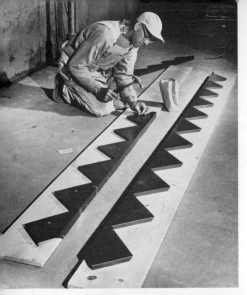

Factory-made steel stair stringers, by Belco, are nailed to the wood sides. Any number of treads may be added, as necessary.

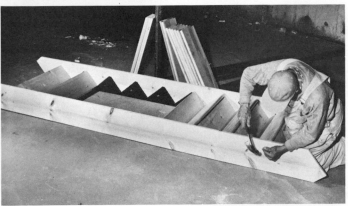

After the ends are sawed to conform with the floor angle, treads and risers are fitted between the stringers, and attached to the steel stair form.

Stair treads are nailed also to the risers, for firm footing. Note that steel form is completely covered.

Dowels take the place of hand rails for basement staircase, for both novelty effect and to offer a feeling of open space. Dowels are easily removed to permit entry of large articles into room.

Clothes-pole dowels are drilled for smaller pegs seated into the stair stringer.

With all the dowels removed, the stairway is clear its entire length, so large panels or equipment can be easily maneuvered.

**Steel spiral stairs.** These are a practical solution where no other stairs can be used because of space limitation or some obstruction that prevents an adequate overhead clearance. Prefabricated spiral stairs are only 24 inches in diameter, requiring a rough floor opening at the top of only 2 inches additional clearance at each side. The inside tread width of the stairs is 21 inches.

The spiral stairs are of steel construction (a desirable fire protection) with 1¼-inch wood treads. The design of the stairs is ornamental, with attractive hand railing and balusters. Sturdy, welded construction makes the treads feel solid underfoot so that not even a timid person would be concerned in using the stairs.

New staircase installed against side wall to provide greatest amount of clearance at the floor level. Space under the stairs is framed out for storage shelves.

Staircase ends on raised platform allowing entry to either side of basement, thus avoiding the massive support column straight ahead of the stairs.

The price for the unit is fairly steep, about from $360 to $600 complete, compared with less than $160 for a well-built wood stairway. But if you're cramped for space, and this is the only practical solution, the price is well worth the very novel and effective result that will be obtained.

One thing to keep in mind, though, is that it would not be possible to bring large plywood or wall-board panels down these stairs, and some other entry method would have to be devised, such as through an enlarged basement window.

**Outside basement stairs.** Construction of an outside entrance may be the first major step in finishing a basement room, so you can bring in the lumber, plywood panels, and other materials needed for the job. In many homes, the only stairway to the basement is a narrow inside arrangement that does not allow enough clearance to carry through large materials.

The outside staircase later will be important for the workshop, permitting materials and your finished projects to be carried in and out. Youngsters can gather for scout meetings and other events without traipsing through the upstairs rooms. The open stairway providing an additional access to the backyard permits storing garden tools handily indoors, and barbeque sessions can be supplied more easily from the basement.

Areaway entrances to the basement once were standard in all homes, mostly for bringing in coal to the bins, but for a long time they have been omitted as unnecessary. With the resurrection of the cellar space for many family uses, the entranceway has proven its value again.

A long step in making the outside entrance more practical and attractive is the prefabricated steel hatch over the steps. These doors are easy to open, have greater head clearance at the stairway, are neat in appearance and effectively protect the basement from rainwater entrance. They may be used to replace the old-time wood doors which were so unsightly and tended always to look rotted.

Where there is no present outside entry, one may be put in. This job may be done for you by a contractor, but many a homeowner has done this work himself, with completely satisfactory results. The hatch and doors come in complete units for installation over the prepared stair opening.

The project involves making an opening in the basement wall, excavating an outside area about 4 by 5 feet in length and width, and a depth of 7 feet. The excavated area is lined with masonry on three sides, and the steps are put in. These are built up from two steel stringers which are attached to the masonry wall, slotted to receive treads cut from 2-by-10 lumber. The steel hatch cover is attached with masonry bolts through the side flanges.

Select a suitable place for the stairs which is satisfactory from both inside and outside. Start with the outside excavation. The stairs will occupy a minimum 4-foot, 6-inch distance from the house wall, and 3-foot, 4-inch span across the front opening. The masonry will be concrete blocks, 8 inches wide, so add 16 inches to the width for the two side walls, and 8 inches to the length across the front. Thus, make the excavation extend 6 feet from the house, and a little over 4 feet in width. Dig to the level of the basement floor, which will be above the footing.

Outside stairway to basement is constructed by opening a wall at backyard position. Foundation opening is made with air hammer in about an hour.

The opening is enclosed with cement blocks on both sides. The earth is banked along the front end for the stairs, which may be either masonry or prefabricated steel.

The wall opening is broken by a concrete contractor with a pneumatic drill. A concrete block wall can be opened in about fifteen minutes, while a poured concrete foundation will take less than an hour, so you see that the cost will come to somewhere between $50 and $100 depending on the distance the contractor has to bring his equipment.

The homeowner can readily open a concrete block wall himself with a cold chisel and sledge, taking perhaps three or four hours of work. Opening a

Steel hatch doors over the stairs are waterproof, easily opened, provide access to basement room directly from backyard.

poured concrete wall by hand sledging should not be attempted, because of the danger of cracking the foundation, unless a series of deep and closely spaced holes are drilled. This would be a tedious and time-consuming job, probably using up half a dozen carbide-tipped drills in the process, so that it is better to let a concrete contractor do it. See that there is sufficient head room at the lower doorway, at least 7 feet.

The masonry walls and door installations are not too difficult, and can be handled by the homeowner. Put in a concrete footing, about 6 inches deep, around the three sides of the excavated areaway. When the concrete has cured, proceed to lay the concrete blocks, plumb and with level courses, lining the three walls. Continue to grade level, then add enough height to be 3 or 4 inches above grade by casting a concrete curb around the opening. When the hatch doors are installed, caulk around the base, in front of the sill, and against the house wall for both weather protection and heat retention.

The stairs are built from two steel stringers which are attached at uniform angles onto the side walls, then lengths of 2-by-10 lumber are inserted into channels for the treads. A plywood panel may be placed on the underside of the stairs.

The door opening in the inside wall is trimmed with a door buck. Any crude spaces between the buck and the original wall left by the air hammer are filled and smoothed with mortar, and the door hung in the frame.

**Enlarging windows.** There's no reason to retain unusually small windows that give a claustrophobic feeling. Substitute large fixed-pane glass for more light and openness. Enlarge the opening by cutting away part of the foundation wall. Increase the size of the window well outside to conform. A window

41

Seepage through foundation wall usually can be corrected by plugging all vulnerable spots with hydraulic mortar. Coating entire wall with special masonry paint will help seal porous concrete.

More serious seepage problems are corrected by excavating a trench along the outside foundation wall, and laying in drain tile connected to a sump or dry well.

Coating exterior of foundation wall with special waterproofing compound will seal the wall against water seepage. The asphalt-base coating is made by U.S. Gypsum Company. Apply with stiff bristle brush.

42

in a concrete foundation can be enlarged quickly by a contractor with an air
hammer, though if the opening is not very large, it can be done by first drilling
a series of deep holes in the concrete around the intended new opening, then
splitting the concrete with a cold chisel or a percussion hammer in an electric
drill. The pre-drilled holes will prevent the concrete from cracking in an unde-
sired direction.

**Heating.** If the cellar now seems chilly, remember that the addition of
wall paneling in the finishing project will help make the room more comfortable. The furnace will provide more heat for the basement if louvered openings,
neatly covered with perforated metal, are made in the furnace-room partition.

If there is a steam system, and some of the feed lines pass along the ceiling
joists, the addition of metal radiation fins along the pipes will help raise the
temperature of the room during the heating season.

Hot water systems with circulating pump can be arranged to feed two or
more radiators in the basement, but this installation should be done by a
plumber or heating contractor, unless you have sufficient experience in this
work, as otherwise the entire home system can be thrown off balance and fail
to function properly. Hot-air ducts can be opened with additional louvers
where necessary to improve the basement heating. If these measures are not
enough, the addition of a couple of electric zone heaters will make the room
comfortable.

**Furnace in the way?** In older houses, furnaces were usually placed without
thought to the possibility of using the basement space for a room. If the heating
plant is located in such a way that it prevents full use of a selected area, it
may be possible to shift it out of the way. Because the connecting water and
steam lines, or hot air ducts, must be taken down and reassembled, this may be
a fairly expensive proposition, running between $300 and $600 in most cases.
A heating contractor can give you a fair price for the shift.

**New compact boilers.** A very old furnace, especially a coal burner converted to fuel oil and not likely to last much longer, might not warrant such
an expenditure. Instead, you might consider junking it and getting one of the
new compact types which are more efficient and trouble-free, take up very
little space, and can be installed in a new location to leave your basement floor
clear for finishing. Thus you accomplish two purposes, without additional cost.
Cost of a completely new boiler or furnace may run about $800, installed.

If moving the furnace makes it possible to utilize the basement for a playroom, then this expenditure seems well worth while because the recreation room
in the basement will be far less costly than any other form of house addition,
and you will most likely obtain more practical room space in the basement than
you can by any other method.

**Low ceiling.** Excavation of a shallow basement to the depth of a foot or
more will increase head clearance without risk to the foundation footings. Care
must be taken to excavate so that the soil below the footings will not slough
out during the digging operation. If the excavation reaches to the bottom of
the footings, a new concrete barrier is poured in a trench all around the walls
into forms pegged along the inside, about a foot from the present foundation.
This entire operation is difficult, and should be done only by an experi-

enced concrete firm. The original concrete floor must be broken up by sledge hammers or an air-powered drill. Just removing this concrete debris and excavated earth by bucketsful is a tiresome task, and requires a dump truck. Another detail is that any supporting columns may have to be reset on new footings, without disturbing the floor joists above.

**New column footing.** This involves setting up temporary supports which are brought to just the right tension so that the original column can be taken out. A new column footing is poured to a depth of one foot deeper than the level of the new floor.

A new support, bolted through a flange to a bottom steel plate, is adjusted by means of its threaded pipe end until it fits tightly against the floor joist, and the temporary supports are removed. A new concrete floor will be laid. This entire process can be done by most concrete contractors, and a firm bid should be obtained for the job. Cost will vary widely depending on the extent of work involved, the difficulty in removing the excavated material, and the size of the new floor. An expenditure of $1,500 or more would be justified, as it would correct a basic deficiency of the house and would enable you to make use of a considerable amount of good living space.

If it is necessary to go down more than a foot to get a ceiling clearance of at least 6 feet 8 inches, the footings can be protected with poured concrete buttresses set at an angle of 30 degrees, pitched down from the foundation walls on banked earth to the new inside grade. The slabs, reinforced with steel rods, are poured to 6-inch thickness, in sections 5 feet long.

The earth is exacavated in staggered 5-foot-long areas along the original footings, allowing each poured slab to set before the next section is excavated. The new concrete floor that is later poured in the basement helps to lock in the lower ends of the slabs against movement, and forms a watertight seal.

A simple effort like connecting gutter downspouts to large clay pipes that drain the water away from the house foundation often solves vexing dampness problem.

It is even possible to obtain ample headroom in a basement where the present ceiling height is only 4 or 5 feet. This poses a difficult and expensive operation as the floor must be excavated about 3 additional feet, far below the depth of the original footings. Therefore, an extended footing must be cast beneath the present one. This work is done from the exterior side in sections of a few feet at a time, by excavating at the outside wall, to a maximum depth of 4 feet below the original footing. A new footing is laid at the bottom, then the foundation wall extended. The exposed part of the old footing plate is broken off with a cold chisel, the part underneath is cleared of soil to the necessary depth, and wood forms set in place for pouring concrete. Free-flowing concrete is poured into the form and allowed to cure before the wood form is removed and the soil backfilled. The cellar floor then is excavated to the predetermined depth, and recemented.

**Covering soil lines.** Basement eyesores like the cast-iron soil pipe and heating pipe should be hidden from view so they won't detract from the appearance of your room. Enclose the soil pipe with wall panels to look like a miniature closet, with a door so you can get at the cleanout plug when necessary. Overhead ducts or water pipes can be boxed in with lengths of wallboard remnants, over framing of 1-by-3 strips, or if the pipes are close to the ceiling, cover the frame with ceiling tiles cut to fit and cemented in place.

Steam pipes will supply extra heat to the basement when the boxlike framing is covered with perforated steel or aluminum panels, trimmed along the outside edges with right-angle corner mouldings. Similarly, openings cut in the furnace room partition can be finished neatly with perforated metal inserts and the opening trimmed with bead moulding like a picture frame.

Wood support beams across the ceiling can be treated simply with a covering of wall paneling material, tacked directly to the beam. In the case of a steel girder, however, a frame of 1-by-3 strips is formed to attach a decorative covering.

**Disguising columns.** Lally columns can't be moved out of the way without proper shoring of the ceiling beams, so it's best to disguise them. They can be boxed in with boards to form a square. A popular way is to wind heavy rope or plastic material all the way up the column, achieving an interesting effect. Or you might try converting the pole into a tree trunk, adorned with mock branches.

**Storage areas.** Plan for specific purposes. A deep but narrow alcove, for instance, would be excellent for receiving extra bridge tables and chairs, or dining table extension inserts. Lumber and other shop supplies should be stored sparingly, if at all, in the house. Better provide a place in the garage or an outside steel shed for lumber storage. Paints, solvents, and similar materials certainly are hazardous and should be kept in a cool place, preferably outside the house, in a storage shed. In any event, store paint cans in a ventilated space, so that any volatile fumes can escape.

**Stall shower.** You can set up a stall shower wherever there is a drain, or where a drain and trap set into the basement floor will not be below the level of the soil pipe leading to the sewer trap.

A prefabricated steel shower, in kit form, costs about $260 including the shower head and faucets, but without the glass door. The receptor pan of the shower must be fitted to the floor drain with a pipe nipple that extends 1 inch into the pan outlet. If the floor trap has a threaded cap, this can be removed and a coupling screwed on the end to receive a nipple cut to the right length. If there is no nipple, one must be inserted and sealed with oakum and lead into the bell end of the floor trap, a job that is best done by a plumber.

Also, hot and cold water lines must be brought in and connected to the faucets. The shower stall is easily assembled, and can be framed in for covering on the outside with wall panels or knotty pine boards. This enclosure can be made large enough at one end to provide a dressing room in conjunction with the shower.

**Finnish sauna baths.** Fortunate indeed is the family that possesses one at home to enjoy this relaxing luxury regularly and conveniently. A sauna is a small room with wood or tile walls and wood benches or bunks. The room is heated by means of a powerful electric stove to high temperatures, about 200 degrees, but with minimum vapor in contrast to the stifling atmosphere in steam baths. The high heat starts profuse perspiration, which cleanses the skin and relaxes tensions.

Sauna rooms are available as complete precut kits, which you can put up in the basement or attic as part of your recreation room program. The kits and necessary equipment are manufactured and sold by Cascade Industries, Inc., Edison, New Jersey; Viking Sauna Corp., 168 S. Van Brunt Avenue, Englewood, N. J. and 2095 Union Street, San Francisco, California, and other regional offices; and Cecil Ellis Sauna, Inc., 18 West 56 Street, New York.

A sauna room for home use is usually quite small, about 6-by-8 feet, or even less. Construction is with thick, interlocking cedar planks, which serve as insulation to keep the heat in. Regular 1 inch tongue-and-groove boards may be used for enclosing the room over 2-by-4 framing studs, with 3-inch fiberglass insulation batts and inside wall covering of Sheetrock panels. The floor also is of planks over 2-by-4 sleepers.

The electric heater, controlled by a thermostat, shuts itself off when the desired temperature is reached. Benches of thick 2-inch redwood or cedar are built into the room for relaxing under the spell.

# CHAPTER FIVE

# FINISHING AN ATTIC ROOM

THE ATTIC offers a promising area for improvement into a teenage recreation room. This would ease the space pressure for the rest of the family, providing extra play and study facilities, plus plenty of huge wardrobe closets. Ranch houses, Cape Cods, and bungalows with high-peaked roofs usually have the largest and most adaptable attics.

This is a project that the handyman can do almost entirely by himself. Attic finishing can be the lowest cost expansion project you can make; that is, if the upstairs loft is of sufficient size, has ample head clearance over a large

A remodeled attic room for hobbies and relaxation provides a welcome retreat for the older folk, as well as the children. Complete with stereo and TV, a comfortable reading space, and facilities for hobbies and work, this area offers parents an ideal hideaway. Floor is covered with Armstrong sheet vinyl.

Attics provide the perfect means for expansion when the family begins to outgrow its living space. This example shows an attractive den for two youngsters, with built-in counters for work and play. Armstrong acoustical ceiling and the insulated floor help to hush the occasional youthful scuffles.

area of at least 7 feet 6 inches, windows for air and light, a regular stairway, and floor joists of adequate load strength. Electric and water connections are near at hand, easily extended at low cost, even for an extra bathroom.

Any deficiencies can be wholly corrected. Installing a stationary or folding stairway, opening additional windows in the side walls, or providing small dormers or perhaps a skylight, involve little difficulty and only modest expense. Strengthening of floor beams is quite complicated because the cramped quarters will not permit fitting single lengths all the way across to the end plates, but a few double joists at critical points will reinforce the floor.

**Watch your head.** Low head clearance, or insufficient interior headroom, will require raising the roof to form a shed dormer along one side of the attic. This is not as costly as it sounds. Often, a shed dormer is formed merely by lifting the entire section of the roof intact to a height of 4 to 6 feet, and supporting it at the new level with framed posts and studs.

Roof-raising may more than double the usable space. This work may take a few days, so be sure to protect your house from unexpected rain by covering the exposed floor area with tarpaulins.

There are indeed some drawbacks to attic rooms, chief of which are noise, excessive heat in the summer, extreme cold in the winter. Proper insulation and a good heating unit can take care of the cold, even in the most bitter winter; air conditioners will keep the room comfortably cool on the hottest summer days.

Another example of comfortable and safe play space in the finished attic. Sloped ceiling is of plywood panels. Walls have built-in storage areas for toys and personal items.

Growing family lived in cramped quarters while all this space in the attic was unused, until a renovation project was started to provide a room at the top.

Maximum utilization of the attic is obtained when the roof is raised at one side to form a shed dormer, thus providing improved head clearance and minimizing the sloped ceiling areas. Photograph shows start in erecting the dormer framework.

Shed roof completely frames and covers while the original roof still remains intact. In some situations, the original rafters are raised to the desired height.

Shed roof framing allows for large picture windows to obtain sufficient daylight. Old roofing is removed when the new structure is completed so there is no problem of damage from interim rainfall.

Noise can be a nuisance, particularly if the room is directly above bedrooms or areas in general use, but there are ways to alleviate the noise problem. Much depends on whether the room will be used by exceedingly active young boys, or by more decorous young girls. Acoustical ceiling tiles and sound-absorbing wall panels cannot help very much, as they serve more to soften sounds within a room than as a barrier to noise transmission through walls or floor. However, a special insulation technique, discussed later, and thick carpeting will do much to reduce this difficulty.

**Planks on joists.** When you climb up to look over the upstairs situation, watch your step if there's only a narrow catwalk over the floor joists. If your foot slips it can go right through the insulation and the plaster ceiling below.

For a closer inspection, it would be a good idea to bring up a few long boards or 4-by-4 panels of ¾-inch commercial grade plywood and lay them across the joists temporarily so you can move around safely. That is, if the ends of the panel are right on the beam. Otherwise it will dip and throw you. These panels will be used later as part of the complete subfloor.

Examine the size and condition of the floor joists. If they are 2-by-6 beams or better, and do not appear twisted or warped, the floor would be strong enough for a room. The 2-by-6 size, however, is not very sturdy and you may decide that it would be worth some expenditure to reinforce the floor with a half dozen or so additional beams.

These long beams can be hoisted up through a window and laid in at strategic spots along present joists, joining them into pairs with bolts through drilled holes. Any insulation batts in the floor that must be torn up in the

Small window dormer is frequently included in attic project to enlarge the room space and to provide for an additional window. Dormer must be insulated, with air space above its ceiling line.

A complete kit for dormer construction is available, including the double-hung window and all necessary framing members, for fast installation. Dormer is finished on exterior surface with siding to match the house, though roofing shingles often are used for this purpose.

process should be tucked back into the space between the joists. The reinforcement beams must be of the same size as your present joists to retain a uniform floor level.

**Access to attic.** Most homes built in recent decades have no regular stairway leading to the attic. Instead, there usually is a hatch placed in a closet, reached by a straight ladder. For an attic room, a favorable location must be found for a stairway, preferably in a hallway that is wide enough so that it could give up about 3 feet of its width for this purpose, or by sacrificing a closet.

An alternative to a regular stairway is a folding stair, used when there is minimum overhead clearance at the top location, or a sliding staircase opening in a hallway or general purpose room on the floor below.

The folding staircase has a spring balance, is easily opened by pulling down a plywood panel in the ceiling with a short pole having a hook at one end. The jacknifed stairs, in two or three sections, unfolds as it opens into a single length. These stairs are, of necessity, somewhat rickety and quite narrow, only 1½ or 2 feet wide, and rise at a steep angle, but they serve the purpose especially for youngsters, if no other means are possible. The sliding ladder-type stairs are easier to handle and more solid underfoot, but need considerable overhead clearance in the attic.

**Cutting the stair opening.** One of the first things that must be done, then, is to install the staircase. This requires an opening in the attic floor wide enough for the stairs, which will be about 24 inches, depending on the type.

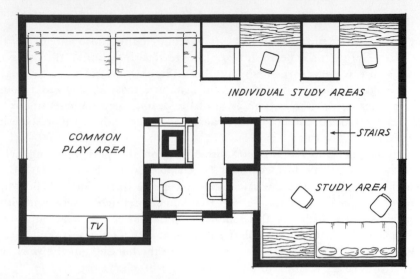

INDIVIDUAL STUDY AREAS

COMMON
PLAY AREA

STAIRS

STUDY AREA

TV

Simple floor plan shows how living, study and sleeping areas are related to each other. Arrangement could be adapted for any attic. Layout works well for two girls and boy, or vice versa, gives each child semi-private area to call his own.

Typical pitched roof receiving a plywood panel section over the packed insulation blankets between the rafters. In this example, panels fit between the rafters, so that the undersides become part of the room design. Panels are nailed to 1-by-2 furring strips attached along the sides of each rafter.

Find a place where such an opening would require cutting into only one of the floor joists. Cut the floor beam in two places to clear a section of the necessary length. You can use a carpenter's saw, but a Stanley electric sabre saw has a special long right-angle offset blade that can cut almost all the way through to the plaster lath at the bottom edge of the beam. Keep the cuts square, so that you can nail reinforcing headers across the open ends of the joists, using the cutout piece for this purpose.

Outline the ladder's trapdoor dimensions on the plaster ceiling below where the door will be located. Drill 1-inch holes at the four corners of the rectangle, for starting the saw cuts along the guide lines. You will find that plaster is an amazing material—so soft that you can scratch or scrape it with a fingernail, yet the cutting of this small section of plaster will wear out two or more hardened saw blades. The plaster is best cut with a tempered keyhole saw, the kind that has extra blades for inserting into the handle, but the work will go faster and easier with a No. 7201 blade in a Stanley sabre saw.

**Anchor the housing.** When the opening is completed, drive four nails through the side joists, the points of the nails just protruding, so they can be driven more deeply with just a tap or two to hold the stair housing.

Lift the closed stair assembly into the opening, so that the covering trapdoor is flush with the lower ceiling, and drive one nail in the assembly housing to partially hold it. With a spirit level, accurately line up the boxlike housing and drive a second nail part way, enough to hold but projecting enough so the nail can be drawn out if necessary. Open the stairs now to test that it is plumb and square, and that the opening mechanism is well balanced.

If all is well, drive additional nails into the housing sides. Finish off the rough ceiling opening with contoured molding along the edges. Place a large eye screw into the trapdoor, and also provide a length of dowel with a hook at the end for engaging the eye screw to pull down the staircase. Keep the stair-opener dowel handy on a wall hook.

**Spiral staircase.** Folding stairs take up about 8 feet of space at both the landing floor and in the attic, so very likely they would crowd a narrow hallway. If an alternative must be found, consider the metal spiral stairs described in Chapter 11. These stairs, which are sensational in appearance, require only a 3½ foot diameter at both top and landing floors, and can easily be installed inside a closet—an ideal situation from a fire safety standpoint since the closet door shuts off updrafts to the attic area, which is a hazard of open stairways. If you will have an attic fan, this spiral staircase installation can serve also as the air current duct when the door is open.

A prefabricated steel spiral staircase of 4, 4½, and 5 foot diameter, complete with 1-inch diameter handrail and choice of platform, may be purchased from the Woodbridge Ornamental Iron Company, 2715 North Clybourn Avenue, Chicago, Illinois 60614. The Econ-Spiral unit is built around a 3½-inch diameter tubular column. Price is about $45 a foot, F.O.B. Chicago. The unit is disassembled for shipment. Measurement is from the lower floor to the floor line at the top, usually 8 to 8½ feet in the average home, or a total cost of about $360 including railing. The stairs may be ordered with the

Spiral stairway is safe and attractive, as well as innovative. Prime purpose is to have a staircase where one otherwise could not be placed, but it is not just a substitute. Staircase can be installed with minimum 4-foot-square floor opening in attic.

Folding attic staircase serves its purpose, though it has to be pulled down and returned to position each time. Children usually do not have any objection to this chore, and even find it's fun. In some situations a folding staircase is the only possibility for attic access.

Joist is cut with carpenter's saw, followed by keyhole saw. In locations where joists are spaced 16 inches apart o.c., it will be necessary to cut through two joists to make opening of sufficient width. Cut through plaster with hardened steel saw or knife.

Plaster, precut through the top, is broken off in section to form a neat rectangular opening in ceiling for stairway.

Cutaway joists are used for reinforcing the remaining joists by nailing section across the open ends, framing the stairway opening.

Staircase shows as a plywood panel, hinged to the frame at ceiling level. Hook is placed on plywood panel to pull down the stairs with a short dowel pole. Trim opening with molding for a neat look.

starting and landing positions to fit the circumstances of your attic setup, and stairs going either to right or left. Also available, at extra cost, are handrails with colorful plastic coating or attractively molded steel, and intermediate wood balusters in several shaped designs. Instead of the safety-plate steel treads, there are plywood, solid wood, and plastic-coated treads at an extra charge.

**Framing the walls.** The finishing process can now be started. First comes framing of the side walls and the new ceiling. The basic techniques of wall and ceiling framing are described in Chapter 12, but there are some specific situations encountered in the attic work. As the rafters are sloped, the ceiling in some part of the room will also be sloped. You will have to decide how far to go when you frame out what are called the knee walls. Generally, an acceptable minimum height here is regarded as 4 feet.

Mark off the positions of the knee walls around the room and put down 2-by-4 plates across the joists along the lines. Cut 2-by-4s into required lengths for the studs, which are attached to each roof rafter and also toenailed to the floor plate. Make sure that these studs are set in plumb and in alignment, so that the finishing wall panels can be fastened to them uniformly. At frequent stages test the stud alignment with a long, straight board, correcting any studs not in line.

**Ceiling collar beams.** The ceiling is framed out with collar beams, also of 2-by-4s, nailed across the rafters at uniform height of at least 7 feet above the floor. Each of the collar beams is reinforced also with a vertical suspension hanger near the center, nailed to a rafter high near the ridge board. If these collar beams are particularly long, over 8 feet, supply two such vertical supports, spaced equally along the beam.

When the wall framing is completed, next stage is that of bringing in the electric cables and any heating lines, such as hot water, tubing, or steam pipes. Wiring for the attic should come from two separate electric circuits, distributed to different parts of the room. Snake the BX cables up through a first-floor closet or other behind-wall area, then run the cables around to the receptacle

57

and fixture positions by threading them through holes drilled in the wall studs, or between the floor joists. Rough in the electric boxes and heating equipment, temporarily connect up the lines.

**Nailing the subfloor.** Now you can proceed to lay down the permanent subfloor of ¾-inch plywood panels or tongue-and-groove flooring nailed to the joists. At this time you should pause to consider a means of cutting down transmission of floor noise—an extra expense but possibly an essential factor in the final success of your attic room.

This consists of covering the entire rough floor surface with insulation batting at least 1 inch thick, and having a density of 3 to 6 pounds per cubic foot. Over the batts, place 2-by-2-inch sleepers about a foot apart, but do not nail them down; rather, allow them to float on top of the insulation blankets where they will eventually compress the insulation fibers to half the original thickness.

A finish floor of ¾-inch plywood is securely nailed to these sleepers, followed by an underlayment of ¼-inch thick Masonite hardboard as a subsurface for the floor tiles. A final contribution to abating the noise nuisance can be thick carpeting over a rubber pad.

**Venting the attic.** The former attic windows are now part of your enclosed room, so new vent openings must be provided in the gables at the peak above the new ceiling. This means cutting into the outside sheathing and siding. You can purchase prefabricated aluminum vent louvers from building supply firms or Sears Roebuck. The openings should be located at opposite sides of the attic space below the ridge board and above the ceiling collar beams.

**Installing insulation.** Knee walls and rafters of the enclosed room area should be insulated with batts or blankets. Full insulation is essential to assure comfort and minimum waste of fuel. For the walls, use insulation blankets at least 4 inches thick with foil-type vapor barrier. The blankets are purchased of the correct width to fit between the studs or joists—either 16 inches or 24 inches on center. Fit the blankets snug between the studs, foil-side facing in toward the enclosed or room area. Attach with a staple gun, spacing the staples no more than 6 inches apart, through the paper side flanges of the blankets.

Do not try to run a continuous blanket across the collar beam, down the rafters and wall. Rather, use separate sections for the collar beam and knee wall to avoid buckling and gaps. Where two ends of the blankets are fitted together, make sure they are butted tightly, or lapped without gaps.

Wherever there is an electrical box, cut the blanket oversize, so the insulation material is compressed tightly against the sides of the box. Similarly with heating and water pipes, make sure the insulation forms a tight seal, with no open gaps.

Any areas that cannot be reached for installing the blankets should be packed with loose vermiculite, poured directly from bags.

The studs and collar beams are positioned according to the original positions of the rafters. You may find that in some instances the distance between framing members is excessive, and the flanges of the insulating blankets won't reach across. Where this occurs, nail long furring strips along the side of the stud or beam to narrow the distance.

Neatly finished attic, though no attempt was made to keep ceiling slopes to minimum. Treatment of corners, however, is unusual and establishes character of the family room.

Always remember that the vapor seal surface of any insulation batt faces inward toward the warm side of the room.

**Three-way switch.** At the stairway, plan to install a three-way switch so that the lights can be turned off within the room as well as from below. This will be useful if the room is used for overnight guests, and generally will mean lower electric bills because forgotten lights can be turned off from below.

Another helpful detail would be some sort of call system for those using the attic room, whether it is an annunciator bell worked off the doorbell transformer, a telephone extension, or a regular intercom. This will preclude the need for shouting through the house to call youngsters for dinner or give them messages. A system of signals based on the number of rings will serve adequately for an ordinary bell.

**A note on windows.** How much window area is desirable for the attic playroom? Small and remote windows. particularly those in deeply recessed shed dormers, are not likely to provide sufficient light or ventilation. On the other hand, excessive window exposure may make an attic room unbearably hot in the summer, difficult to heat in the winter.

A reasonable compromise, with thoughtful location of larger windows in regard to climate conditions, can resolve the question. But keep in mind, too, that former standards and prohibitions no longer apply. Air conditioners and attic fans are fully effective in maintaining a pleasant room temperature, while present-day insulation materials and installation methods are a great improvement in providing home comfort. Space heaters and thermostat controls assure even-temperature comfort in cold weather.

**The case for large casements.** Larger windows are justified on both esthetic and practical grounds. So if you're raising the roof, go all the way and put in plenty of window surface. For light, use casement or double hung windows. A good type for ventilation is the awning window, which is operated by a hand crank and provides maximum protection against rain if left open—an important detail in attic rooms.

Before enlarging or cutting window openings, select your new windows and obtain the dimensions so you can make the rough openings.

**Framing new windows.** First, remove the old window frame, except for one vertical casing and jamb at the side stud where the new window will be located. Next, remove the exterior clapboard to make the opening of the required size. If your siding is aluminum, cut away just enough so that there will be room for an end cap, finish trim and channel. Remove wall shingles for about a foot beyond the lines of the new opening.

Construct the rough window frame on the inside with double studs and header, then cut through the wall sheathing, using the inside surface of the rough frame as a guide. Nail in the new window, shimming it where necessary so it is plumb and square. Pack open spaces between frame and studs with insulation fibers or vermiculite.

Fit the sash, nail in window stops, trim, and base. On the outside, tack building paper over the exposed sheathing, replace siding or shingles, and install bent flashing metal over the drip cap.

**Extra bathroom.** While perhaps not essential, a bathroom in the attic room is a worthwhile investment, particularly if the room will be used for putting up occasional overnight guests. The cost of a bathroom installation in the attic probably will be less than for one located anywhere else, because of easy access to the plumbing lines and nearness of the vent stack.

Locate the new bathroom directly above or just to a side of the present bathroom in the floor below, so that all plumbing lines will be at the closest distance. A washstand and toilet are sufficient for a playroom, but include a shower or tub if the attic room possibly will be used for guests. The bathroom installation would best be done by a licensed plumber.

Enclose the facility with partitions of 2-by-4 studs, finishing the inside walls with Marlite plastic-coated panels, which are resistant to moisture and are recommended for bathroom use. If the bathroom is so located that no window can be provided, install a ventilator fan and duct leading to the outside.

**Wall finishing.** Lowest cost finishing materials are gypsum sheetrock panels for the walls, acoustical tiles for the ceiling. Either walls or ceiling may be done first. Additional popular wall materials are tongue-and-groove knotty pine boards, ¼" prefinished plywood. Masonite's prefinished Royalcote hardboard paneling in a selection of fine wood grains and other finishes, and for luxury, Weldwood plywood or Marlite plastic-coated panels.

Wallboard installation is described in Chapter 12. For attics, the panels are nailed to the knee walls, then the sloped area above, with batten or channel moldings at the midway joints.

For the ceiling tiles, 1-by-2 furring strips are nailed along the collar beams, spaced according to the size of the tiles. The acoustical tiles are attached with a staple gun as described in Chapter 12. Many panel manufacturers make available moulding trim to match the finishes of the wall panels.

One problem in wall finishing is that of bringing the large 4-by-8 panels into the attic if there is only a minimum stairway opening. If you're having the roof raised for a shed dormer, that is the time to bring up all needed materials, including a sufficient number of wall panels, through the wide-open area. If no roof-raising will be done, and no opening of 4-foot width can be arranged, you might have to restrict the wall finishing to knotty pine boards, which are only 8 inches wide and do not present any such problem.

You might also include a plentiful array of built-in chests and bookcase units, recessed between the wall studs. These shelves or chests of drawers can be purchased completely assembled in lumberyards, ready for finishing. If these units are set into the wall frame, be sure to insulate the areas behind them.

**Partitioning.** The attic room may be a lot larger than you want for a single room. If that is so, the space can be partitioned to form one or more smaller rooms, including a guest room. But try to plan the arrangement so that it is not necessary to go through one room to reach the other. A small entryway at the head of the staircase providing entrance to either room is the ideal setup.

**Lay the flooring.** One of the final steps is to put down the finish flooring of resilient tiles, cemented with paste to the hardboard underlayment, as described in Chapter 12. Also remaining are molding trim, ceiling fixtures, and electric receptacle plates.

**Heating equipment.** Don't stint on the heating if you want the new attic playroom to be comfortable and used regularly. The regular house heating plant nearly always can be used to handle the extra space whether the heater is steam, hot water, or hot air.

But in some cases you may want to install separate gas or electric space heaters to provide instant heat. Steam heat will be the most difficult to bring up, as it means cutting in on lower lines to connect a radiator and the return. Hot water tubing, however, is quite simple to handle, the fittings easily joined by sweat soldering.

**Storage areas.** Though the areas behind the knee walls are quite low overhead, there is considerable space that is excellent for storage purposes, particularly for out-of-season garments, sports equipment, luggage, etc. The floor and walls in the spaces under the eaves therefore should be finished with tightly fitted panels so they are clean, dust-free, and neat. Remnants from large panels used for the recreation room walls can be used up in this way. Set across doors up in your knee walls. If there is a large full-height space at some job or ell in the attic, you might want to make a luxurious wardrobe closet lined with aromatic cedar. Be sure to wire any storage areas and closets for individual light bulbs, and include automatic door switches so that you won't have to worry about whether you remembered to turn off the lights.

Cedar boards, ⅜ inch thick and in random lengths, are sold in bundles containing material to cover 32 square feet of surface. The cedar boards are tongue-and-groove, not only along the sides but on the ends as well, so that the random lengths are easily linked together, end-to-end, in strips when attached to the wall frame.

Construction starts with 2-by-4 framing for the walls and ceiling, taking in the full available area, regardless of its shape, to obtain a wardrobe of the largest possible size. Any irregular sections of the closet can be utilized with shelves for hat boxes and storage of other accessories.

Tack building paper over the inside portions of the frame, as a dust sealer. Install the strips first across the ceiling members. There need be no concern about having the ends of each strip fall on a frame member to be nailed down, as the tongue-and-groove ends of continuing boards will interlock. Start at one end of the top, nailing the strips first all the way across the ceiling beams, then do the second course all across, proceeding in this manner until the entire top is covered.

For the walls, start at the bottom, install the strips in rows with 4d nails driven through the face of the wood into the wall studs. When cutting excess lengths at the end of each course, be sure to include the depth of the groove with your measurement, so the strip butts tightly against the end wall. Tap the pieces together lightly as you go, so that the joining tongues-and-grooves are fully seated.

If there are any open spaces at the corner joints, seal them with quarter-round moldings. For maximum mothproofing value, you might want to finish the floor as well with the aromatic cedar, laying in the strips at the far corner and working toward the front.

Be sure to include an electric light with automatic door switch in the closet. When the cedar lining is completed, fit the closet with clothes hanger rods and shelves for shoes, hats, and other items. An important detail is to make the door as tightly sealed as possible, using rubber weatherseal strips that are set so they become compressed as the door is closed. The cedar eventually will lose much of its original natural aroma, but this can be renewed with periodic spraying of cedar oil. As an additional precaution against moths, keep sacks of paradichloride crystals in the wardrobe to permeate the closet with the insect repellent.

# CHAPTER SIX

# CONVERTING A GARAGE

AN ATTACHED garage, one that is part of the house itself, is particularly adaptable for converting into a recreation room. Low cost is one distinct advantage—the structure is essentially complete, having walls, roof, and floor. Electrical and heating, even the plumbing lines if you want to add a serving buffet or bar sink, are close by for easier installation. The prime decision, then, would revolve on what is more important to you—a roof over your car, or a sizable playroom for your family. As to the car, very likely you can find a suitable spot to put up a protective carport which would be an adequate substitute.

Some houses have double garages for two cars, offering the possibility for a sensationally spacious recreation room, or the open area can be divided with a partition for a one-car garage with a single overhead door, leaving the rest for living space. Garage dimensions nearly always are quite adequate, usually 20 or more feet long and with a width of at least 12 feet.

Given that much length, a small area at one end can be set aside and partitioned for a separate room with an outside door to store a lawnmower and other garden tools.

When the garage door is replaced with regular clapboard or shingles, your home will look much larger and more attractive.

**Floor level.** The project is greatly simplified if the garage floor is somewhat below the level of the house floor, the roof line is integral with that of the house, and the garage is so situated in relation to the house rooms that a connecting door will lead into the new room from a hallway or kitchen.

Overhead clearance generally is more than ample except perhaps in situations where there is a room above the garage. But even here, the inside height of the garage is often greater than that within the house itself because the garage would be at grade level.

Building up the floor of the garage sacrifices less than 6 inches of the overhead clearance, so that even if the ceiling height is only 8 feet, there would remain at least the 7½-foot height which should be regarded as the acceptable minimum.

**Height for ceiling.** Determine ceiling clearance not by the height of a peaked roof, but rather by the distance from floor to where the rafters meet the walls. It is at that point the joists will be placed for the ceiling. There is,

Garage looked like this before it was converted into a recreation room as part of the house by installing a floor and ceiling, finishing the walls, and replacing the door with wall siding.

Converted garage becomes an attractive room. Extra window was installed in rear wall. Room is heated with hot air registers. Wall paneling is Masonite Royalcote. Powder room was included in the addition.

however, an alternative that would increase overhead height a foot or more. That is to place the collar beams above the position of the rafter plates.

This method would result in a sloped ceiling for a short distance on two sides of the room, which might be of interesting appearance rather than objectionable. Occasionally, garages are found with a sparse 10-foot width, which would be somewhat inadequate for a room. Alteration work for a 4- or 6-foot widening is practical providing the lot line permits such extension at that side.

Erecting a new exterior wall and refinishing with siding would not be very expensive. The cost would be affected by whether the roof over the additional width will be somewhat below the original roof line, following the same styling, or the added section become part of an extended roof of the entire house. This need not mean an entire reshingling job, however, as only a narrow continuous strip of the original shingles need be torn up to merge the new section.

**New gutters.** If the small roof section is separate and at a lower level, it can have its own short rain gutter into which the longer original one can flow. Combining the added roof part with the house roof will most likely require a complete replacement with a new gutter extending the entire width.

A possible drawback to the project may be where the entire inside garage wall abuts the wall of a bedroom, creating the question of family access to the new recreation room. Several possibilities are offered as solutions. One is to partition off a narrow end of this bedroom to provide a corridor from the hallway directly to the recreation room. Another is to utilize a closet at the corner of the bedroom, for a pass through, breaking into the wall for a doorway from the corridor. A substitute closet can be provided at another part of the bedroom.

A more complex solution is to build an enclosed balcony as a passageway around the outside of the house, designed to look like a breezeway. There's no reason why the balcony need be so obtrusive as to detract from the appearance of the house, particularly if it is built at the rear or side. This added construction, however, would considerably increase the total cost of the project.

**Work schedule.** Main steps in the converting project would include removal of the overhead door, cutting openings in the side and rear wall for new windows, laying a wood floor at a height equal to the house floor level, framing the open outside wall to replace the garage door and the other walls for paneling, placing beams for the ceiling, insulating the entire room, bringing in electric cables, and cutting a doorway into the interior house wall. Finally, there is the finishing, which involves installing the windows and door, putting up the wall panels, ceiling tiles, electric fixtures, and laying the surface floor. Then the built-in units are added, at your leisure.

Almost all of this work can be done by a willing homeowner. An especially favorable aspect of this project is that there's a roof overhead to start with, so that the work can progress as rapidly or slowly as you wish, and you can devote whatever free time is available to do each stage.

Before you start, a few preliminary details require attention. The concrete floor may have large grease stains from the car crankcase. These should be thoroughly cleaned to remove a source of unpleasant odor that would penetrate

Covered car port at side of house is enclosed for a family room. The patio, put in at time house was built, has roof integral with that of house.

Note that patio floor is three steps down below floor level inside house. With the new wood floor raised about 10 inches, the room will require two steps down at the inside entrance. Original door is retained in project for economy purposes.

Completed room with bay window at front merges well into the house lines. Siding matches that on the rest of the house.

the recreation room. Scrub the floor with a strong detergent, preferably the kind used by service stations to clean pavements.

**Seal floor drain.** If there is a floor drain in the garage, seal it off with a cap to prevent sewer gas from rising after water in the trap has evaporated. If the drain does not have a threaded nipple for the cap, consult your plumber for the best way to dispose of the drain. One method that is commonly used is to plug the nipple with okum or cement mortar, over which melted lead is poured to seal the opening.

An exterior garage wall that is of masonry construction, particularly concrete blocks which are subject to considerable moisture penetration, should be waterproofed on the inside surface with a coating of asphaltum to protect the wall paneling that will be put up to finish the room.

The garage project might well start with building a wood floor. Garage floors almost always are at a lower level than the house floor, and it is desirable to have both at the same level. This can be done if there is sufficient ceiling height, otherwise a stepdown into the converted recreation room would not be objectionable.

**Floor sleepers.** Sleepers of 2-by-4 or 2-by-6 lumber are laid on edge, lengthwise and 12 inches apart on center, located so that the edges of 4-foot-wide plywood panels always fall on the center for nailing. If the wood floor is raised a foot or more, use 2-by-8 lumber, laid across supporting beams placed along the far walls. The lumber should be of good quality, kiln dried and straight, so that the supports will be uniformly flat.

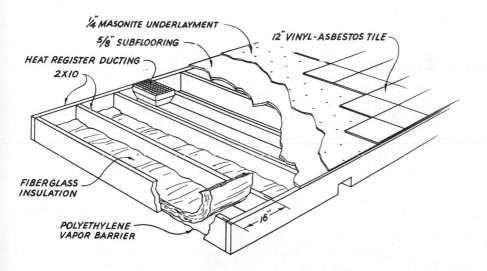

Details are shown for garage conversion project. Floor is first thoroughly cleaned to remove old grease stains, then built up with 2-by-10 sleepers to make floor level with that of the adjoining room. Heat ducts are placed between the floor sleepers, which are well insulated.

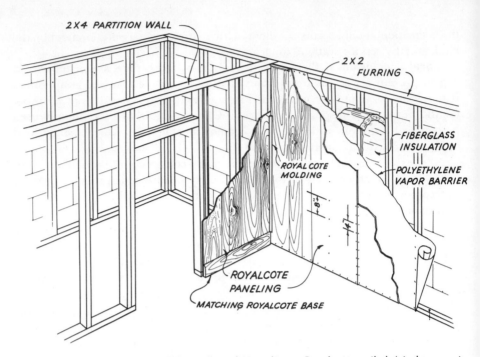

Details of partition framing and the wall insulation shown. Panels are nailed 4 inches apart along edges, 8 inches apart along center line, except when installed with adhesive bead on framing members.

In place of standard 2-by-3 or 2-by-4 studs, walls may be framed out with 1-by-4 furring strips, attached directly to the masonry wall with special fasteners. Furring must be shimmed where necessary for straight and uniform lines, and vertical pieces inserted between the furring for nailing the panel edges.

The concrete garage floor will have a slight pitch, and this must be compensated for by shimming the sleepers so they are precisely level—there's no point in starting with a tilted floor! You might also put in spacer braces between the sleepers to keep them in alignment.

When arranging the sleepers, leave sufficient space at the front of the garage, where the door will be removed, for the plate on which the wall studs will be placed when the door is removed, so that the stud plate is directly on the concrete rather than on the wood floor, and the plate closes the ends of the sleepers.

Insulation of the floor comes next. Use 4-inch-thick fiberglass insulation batts for 12-inch spacing. Fit the insulation blankets snug between the sleepers, stapling the side flanges to the wood members. When the ends of two batts are joined, make sure that they are tightly butted. Place the insulation with the vapor side up, facing the inside of the room, so that vapor does not penetrate and become trapped within the insulation material. Narrow spaces along walls, or between two sleepers that have to be placed closely together, should be packed with vermiculite granules poured into the opening and spread evenly.

**Temporary catwalk.** Place wood planks or plywood panels temporarily over the floor sleepers so you can move around without disturbing the insulation.

Now take down the old garage door, remove its mechanism and the door moldings. Frame out the opening with 2-by-4 studs, and include rough openings for any windows. Nail up sheathing boards or insulation panels on the exterior over the studs. If the outside framing plate is at grade level and therefore subject to termite attack, place a metal termite shield under the framing plate, and tightly caulk the bottom joint.

The inside walls also are prepared for paneling. Possibly these walls already have stud framing, even a wall covering of sheetrock or asbestos. If the wall is plumb and straight, the finishing panels may be applied over it with adhesive and nails. The chances are, however, that this garage wall is not perfectly straight, and will need furring strips, carefully shimmed, to provide a suitable surface.

**Furring on masonry walls.** If the wall does not have studs, put up a framework of 2-by-4's along the walls. An alternative is to attach 2-by-2 furring directly to the wall with masonry anchors nailed through the furring.

The ceiling is framed with 2-by-4 or 2-by-6 joists, fastened across the rafters at the predetermined level and reinforced with vertical supports, or furring strips laid across the joists as stiffeners. Check on the joists as you go to see that they are all uniformly level and true.

Rough in all necessary electric outlet and lighting fixture boxes, securely nailed to the wall frame, and thread the wire cables to these boxes along the floor and through holes or notches in the studs. Also, put in any heating lines at this time, so that the wall insulation won't have to be disturbed.

Walls and ceiling are insulated with 6-inch fiberglass blankets, stapled between the studs and joists along their paper flanges, the vapor barrier facing inside the room. Wherever electric boxes or other obstructions are encountered, pack the insulation tightly against the fixture or to the stud behind it. If the insulation must be cut to bypass any obstructions, pack open spaces tightly with insulation fibers.

**Framing windows.** While putting up the wall studs, frame out the openings for any windows that will be installed. In this recreation room, a large window in the rear wall, facing the backyard, would be desirable, as this location would normally provide the greatest privacy.

Next, put down the subflooring, which consists of ¾-inch commercial grade plywood in 4-by-4-foot panels. Nail these panels securely to the floor sleepers, placing nails about 3 inches apart so that the floor will not squeak. Cover the panels with heavy building paper, then put down a smooth underlayment of ¼-inch-thick hardboard panels, also in 4-by-4 size, using 1-inch screw-type nails, spaced 3 inches apart in each direction. Allow ¼ inch expansion space between the hardboard panels.

**Cutting an inside door.** The inside door opening is made by cutting through the wall. If you have the original house plans, check them carefully to find the most desirable location for the door, avoiding any hidden pipes or ducts. Mark out the opening, cut through the plaster first, using a carborundum wheel in a portable saw, set to the right depth of cut, or break out the plaster with hammer blows alongside a stud. Avoid excessive breakage as this will mean considerable plaster patching later.

You will have to cut also through any sheathing and outside siding on that wall. In many attached garages, the interior dividing wall is of concrete block. The necessary blocks can be removed after first splitting a block with a cold chisel, and also breaking out half blocks where necessary along the side of the opening.

As this is a bearing wall, lintels must be placed for support above the openings. In the concrete block wall, chop deep gouges on each side along the top for inserting a heavy steel plate or angle iron extending at least 2 inches into each side. Pack mortar into the space between the lintel and the remaining blocks above it, using a narrow joint striking tool to push the mortar in deeply.

**Hanging the door.** In the inside door opening, place a length of 2-by-6 across the top, supported by double 2-by-4 studs on each side. The rough opening for the door should be about 2 inches wider and 1 inch higher than the size of the door, to allow for the door buck. Install the inside door, mortising the

Old garage door and all its hardware is removed, and opening framed with 2-by-4s for outside surfacing, which need not match the original house siding.

Large double garage can be partitioned to retain one side for car storage while finishing the remainder into a den. The partition must be of masonry, such as cement blocks, and the garage part has its own ventilating window. In this instance, a door will have to be opened at one side for access to the house.

hinges, lock and latch plate, and shimming the door buck as necessary so the door hangs plumb and swings easily.

The ceiling joists are prepared for the finish tiles with 1-by-2-inch furring strips, spaced according to the size of the tiles, which may be 12, 16, or 24 inches on center. Installation of the furring will go more quickly if you use a precut spacer strip to align the furring. The tongue-and-groove accoustical tiles are put up with a staple gun.

**Finishing the walls.** Instructions for installation of wall panels are in Chapter 12.

Whatever wall panels you use, precondition them to the room's atmosphere by standing the panels in the room for at least two days before installation. Obtain the correct installation moldings for joining panels at inside and outside corners, edgings, and ceiling cove. For some brands of paneling, matching vinyl-covered wood moldings are available. Instructions for ceiling tile installation are also given in Chapter 12.

The finished floor can now be laid, using any type of resilient tiles, as the wood floor now is above grade.

The remaining steps in the project are putting the outside siding over the

Garage with breezeway makes ideal candidate for remodeling into a practical family recreation room. Garage is just a foot below the floor level of the house, and will be built up so the level is continuous throughout. Garage has ample headroom.

Breezeway is easily enclosed with wall to match the house siding, or with brick to provide variation. In this situation, ceiling height of breezeway will be ample if floor is raised only one foot, with stepdown from the house entrance.

former garage door wall, wiring the electrical connections in the outlet boxes, and installing the heating units.

**Converting a carport.** What if there is no garage, only an overhang of the house roof to form a carport? Well, a room conversion can also be done, but it will cost quite a bit more than would an enclosed garage. The supposition is that in this carport, which is adjacent to the house, the roof overhang is supported by masonry columns, or high metal lally columns.

If the car area is not paved, the first move will be to put down a concrete slab, with a perimeter footing of sufficient depth and strength to support side walls. The footing should be located inside the roof overhang, as far in as you can spare the space, while still leaving enough area for a good-sized recreation room.

**Under the roof.** Also, the footing need not be in line with the supporting columns. Depending on where these are situated, the footing may be within or beyond the line of the columns. In the latter case, the columns would be part of the room where they can be enclosed with the wall panels. As compensation for this, your room would be considerably larger than if it were kept within the column lines.

Build up the slab perimeter with at least one course of 3¾-inch-wide concrete blocks, then continue up to the roof soffit with 2-by-4 stud framing to enclose the room, including the window opening as you go. The wall studs are sheathed on the outside with tongue-and-groove boards or insulation panels.

When installing siding on the new wall, remove some of the original clapboard or shingles so that the new siding spans the joint line of your new room with staggered joints with the result that there is a real match of the old and new sections.

The room is now fully enclosed, ready for the insulation and finishing work. An inside door is cut into the house wall for entrance to the room, and the floor built up with sleepers to approximate level of the house floor and finished with resilient tiles over a plywood subfloor, as described in this chapter and in greater detail in Chapter 12. Wall paneling and ceiling finishing also follow the procedures previously described.

**Taking the breeze out of a breezeway.** If your garage is connected to the house with a breezeway, it will be necessary to completely enclose this area so it becomes a corridor leading to the new playroom. This is fairly simple, but keep in mind that the new corridor will have to be as warm as the room, so there is no "cold passage" between the room and the house.

The breezeway floor should be treated the same as that of the garage, with a wood floor and the same surface tiles. Heating pipes brought to the garage through the breezeway area may provide sufficient heat for the corridor. If your room will have individual space heaters, however, it will be necessary to provide a similar installation for the breezeway corridor.

# CHAPTER SEVEN

# CONVERTING A PORCH

A ROOFED porch is a suitable candidate for conversion into a year-round re-creation room if it meets certain requirements. A prime condition is that the porch have a door leading from the kitchen, dining room, or neutral corridor, or be so situated that a doorway can be opened in a wall to provide access from one of the other rooms of the house.

A conversion job can be done at modest cost, much less than would be involved in starting from scratch to build a complete house addition. How-ever, it would be wasteful to make this investment unless the porch is of ample size, 9'-by-12' or more, and has a stone or concrete floor that is below the level of your house floor, and built with an adequate footing around its perimeter. The roof should be high enough to allow sufficient head clearance after the underside of the roof rafters has been enclosed with ceiling tiles or panels and the floor raised about 4 inches.

**Types of porches.** Some porches are built above grade level with floor joists supported over a crawl space on a masonry foundation, or with the joists supported on masonry or lally columns set upon concrete footings. If in solid condition, such porches can be remodeled and adequately insulated for com-fortable heating.

It is possible to combine a porch with an adjacent room to get a single large recreation room. This is a fairly expensive job as it means tearing down a section of the exterior house wall and putting in a heavy beam or steel girder for load-bearing support. This work must be done by expert craftsmen who have the proper hydraulic jacks to raise the supporting beam under the cor-rect tension so there will be no shift in the supporting walls. This beam, inci-dentally, will bisect the enlarged room, projecting below the ceiling level.

**Replacing the summer porch.** Taking the porch for a family room need not mean the complete loss of a cool summer veranda. The new room can be planned with plenty of window area and large sliding glass doors that will allow sufficient ventilation during the hot summer days, or an effective air condi-tioner can be installed, to serve the original purposes of the porch. Alterna-tively, an awning-covered and screened patio at another part of your garden could substitute for the converted porch. This project can be completely handled by the homeowner at modest cost.

The porch remodeling involves framing the side walls, putting in windows

Bringing a porch inside. The old back porch was of little value compared to the need for living space in this home. Porch walls were enclosed, roof carefully insulated.

By opening section of original wall for pass-through from kitchen, and finishing rest of walls with Masonite Royalcote panels, porch becomes a year-round family room. Serving counter eases traffic in kitchen, which can be closed off with louvered shutters.

and an exterior door if one is desired, insulating and building up the floor with a wood deck, insulating the side walls and underside of the roof rafters, bringing in electric circuits, installing a heating system and air conditioner, finishing the walls with panels, the ceiling with acoustical tiles, and the floor with vinyl sheeting or tiles.

**Prefabricated fireplace.** A fireplace would provide a charming and cheerful focal point for your entertainment center, adding color and supplementing the heating facilities. It would be appreciated no end when storms cut off your power supply and the fireplace becomes the sole source of heating for your home.

A fireplace may cost anywhere from a few hundred to thousands of dollars. Most economical is the prebuilt, Majestic Contemporary model which is wood-burning or gas-fired, costs a little more than $300 in a complete kit including the vent pipes and simulated chimney. The fireplace is free-standing, does not require either a concrete footing or a chimney, as the flue goes through the ceiling and roof and is fully insulated with asbestos for safety.

Large windows retain the open feeling of a porch for the enclosed family room, provide maximum view of the great outdoors. Wood windows with insulating glass assure maximum all-weather comfort.

**Framing porch walls.** First step in the porch remodeling is to frame out the walls. If there is a concrete slab almost at grade level, it would not be advisable to lay down the 2-by-4 wood plates for the wall frame right at the edge of the concrete, as this would invite a hidden invasion of termites. The perimeter of the slab must be built up with concrete blocks, at least one course high.

Use partition size concrete blocks, of 3¾ inches thickness. Lay the block in a mortar bed, compressing the mortar at each joint between blocks with a

Sliding glass doors are popular and practical, provide easy access to backyard, together with maximum daytime view and light. The slicing patio doors have Thermopane insulating glass.

Attractive use of wood imparts a sense of warmth and comfort to converted porch room. Walls have cedar paneling. Sloped roof deck is finished with white pine for interesting contrast.

Early American theme is carried in this room by hooked rugs and pew-style wall bench, with old-time butter churn. The converted porch has brick chimney on inside wall.

Former screened porch enclosed with large wood windows and completely insulated to form a year-round family recreation room. Room is built on concrete block foundation, which was extended to join room with kitchen.

Nighttime exterior view of enclosed porch room, showing window effect and the built-in rotisserie with its hood vented through the roof.

striker tool to assure a tight seal. If there is to be an exterior doorway in the new room, lay in the blocks face down on the slab at the opening, so that the block height will be only 3¾ inches above the concrete—this height will be compensated for by the wood sleepers, which will be placed to build up the floor level.

**Use termite shield.** When the concrete mortar has cured, proceed with the wall framing by placing 2-by-4 wood plates along the outside edge of the blocks, with a termite shield of bent copper or galvanized sheeting between the blocks and the wood plate.

The original porch roof supports at the corners may be retained, but should be reinforced with an additional 2-by-4 in line with the other framing members to permit flush nailing of the wall panels. Also, in framing, pay particular attention to those studs which go against the house wall. These should be secured tightly with long screws or anchor bolts into the walls, and the joint sealed on the outside with caulking compound.

**Buy windows first.** Before the framing goes any further, you should have decided on the type of window, and made the purchase. Obtain the detailed specification sheets so you will know the dimensions for the rough openings to be left in the wall frame for the windows.

Wood exterior doors are standard size, 30 inches wide, 6 feet 8 inches high, and the rough frame allows 2 inches in the width and 2 inches in the height, for the door jambs and the threshold. The framed opening for sliding glass doors should conform to the manufacturer's specifications, including provisions for any special hardware and track channels.

It's important to mark on your plan the location of electric receptacles and switches, and the direction that the circuit wiring will come into the room. Thus you can drill ¾-inch holes in the studs and plates for pulling through the electric BX cable before the studs are nailed up—this will be a lot easier to do than drilling sideways into the studs after they are in place.

Locate the 2-by-4 studs 16 inches apart on centers, but be careful to see that the first stud distant from any wall corner is placed so that its center line is 16 inches from the end wall, rather than from the centerline of the starting stud which is against the wall. If you fail to allow for this, the edge of the 4-foot-wide wall panel will fall short of the stud to which it must be nailed.

Install the windows, using wood wedges to square them into the openings.

Converted porch room with open-style fireplace has embossed linoleum floor with vinyl inserts for accent. Double set of doors leading into the house has photo murals on door glass.

Former screened porch is extended by adding a section of concrete slab, poured between curbings of poured concrete over deep footings.

Corner posts are set solidly into the concrete before slab is poured. This procedure is not required in most instances, the posts being supported directly on the concrete base.

Framing is erected on concrete slab for construction of an enclosed room, retaining the original door leading from the house for entrance to the new room.

Roof rafters are attached to support beam fastened to the house wall to provide uniform pitch for the roof.

Closeup shows double nailing of ceiling joists and roof rafters in the new room.

Next, apply sheathing over the outside, using either wood boards or thick weatherproofed insulating panels nailed to the 2-by-4s and extending down to cover the concrete blocks. Do not butt the sheathing tightly against the window frames, but rather leave about ½ inch space all around. Cover the sheathing with builder's paper.

**Build up the floor.** The floor gets attention next. Lay 2-by-4 wood sleepers. (Use 2-by-6 or even larger lumber if needed to bring the floor to the desired level, preferably equal to that of the house floors.) The sleepers are placed lengthwise 1 foot apart to provide a solid floor base that won't be "bouncy." Make sure the sleepers are at uniform level, using shims where necessary.

Before putting in floor or wall insulation, draw in your electric conduit

Walls of enclosed porch room are covered on the outside with sheathing or insulation board, after the windows are framed. Siding completes the installation.

and the heater tubing, if they will go along the floor or walls, and rough in electrical boxes to connect the wires. Also, if there will be any recessed radiators or an air conditioner, make the required openings in the frame and install the units.

Insulate the floor with vapor-seal rock wool or fiberglass insulation batts, 4 inches or more thick in 12-inch width. Lay the batting between the sleepers, vapor seal side up, (facing the warm side of the floor) so that vapor does not get though and condense underneath onto the concrete. Staple the paper batt flanges along the sides of the sleepers. Insulation must be tightly fitted, ends butted together.

Further details on installing the insulating batts are given in Chapter 9.

For the walls and roof, use rated insulation batts in 16-inch width, stapling them between the wall studs and the roof rafters, always with the vapor side facing inside the room. If the room is to have a ceiling below the rafters, install the horizontal beams and tack the insulation between these beams rather than between the rafters.

The floor decking is ¾-inch plywood, in 4-by-4 panels, of the cheapest commercial grade, nailed to the screeds. Use screw-type nails, and plenty of them, so that the plywood is well secured and won't squeak. Leave about ⅛ inch expansion space between the plywood panels. Over this floor, put down an underlayment of ¼-inch hardboard, also in 4-by-4 panels and nailed down with 1-inch screw-type nails set 3 inches apart in each direction. The floor is now completed except for the resilient tile surfacing, which will be laid after the walls are paneled.

Wall panels are nailed up, fitted around the window and heat-convector openings. Make sure the panels are aligned plumb. The ceiling is prepared for the acoustical tiles with 1-by-2 furring strips, nailed across the beams and spaced either 12 or 16 inches apart on centers according to the dimensions of the tiles. The tongue-and-groove tiles are put up by stapling the wide flanges to the furring. For this you will need a high-compression staple gun that can shoot staples with legs 5/16 inch or longer.

The staple gun can be rented for a day, which is as long as the job should take, at any hardware or lumber dealer, for about $1. When putting up the tiles, fit and align them uniformly without undue pressure that forces the tongues in too deeply, as this will cause bulges and ragged joint lines.

Inside walls are finished quickly with large plywood or coated panels. Shown is Marlite's wormy cypress, with random grooves. Panels must be put up plumb.

**Finishing the job.** Your porch room now begins to take shape, and you can stand back to proudly survey your work. But much more remains to be done.

The exterior surface is to be finished. It's generally better to have the outside siding match the rest of the house. If it is of cedar shingles, clapboard, or board and batten, you might be able to do this part of the work yourself, though it might be better to have it done by an experienced carpenter. In any event, avoid starting the new clapboard all at the joint line of the porch wall; rather, remove some of the original boards so the joints will be staggered as they are in the rest of the wall. If the house has aluminum siding, let the work be done by a regular siding installer, and include in the job aluminum covers for your window frames and sills so they won't need periodic painting. Also remember to put up rain gutters along the roof, if they were not there when the porch was just a porch.

Inside, the final stages will consist of laying the finished floor tiles, putting up cove moldings around the ceiling, and finishing off the rest of the walls with base shoe moldings and trim around the windows. Any outside door should be professionally weatherstripped.

Information on electrical and heating work is given in Chapter 10. If the electrical work is not done by a regular contractor, be sure that it conforms strictly to code requirements, and that you get a certificate of approval from the local building department after the work is completed.

Ceiling tiles are quickly and easily attached to wood furring strips with staples.

# CHAPTER EIGHT

# BUILDING AN EXTENSION

ALMOST EVERY home has enough space in its rear lot so that part of it can be given over for constructing a room addition. Such an expansion at either side of the house often is barred by a narrow lot and the requirement to maintain an open areaway between adjacent houses, but local regulations rarely restrict the taking of 12 or 14 feet from the backyard space for a home addition.

Construction of a complete new wing isn't the overwhelming experience that some people imagine, and it certainly need not be as costly as is pictured by the usual Sunday newspaper feature.

If your house is built so its first-floor level is high above grade, the new room can be supported on masonry piers, thus avoiding all the cost of a foundation wall. A lot that slopes down sharply away from the house actually is an advantage in this instance. In some circumstances, an acutely pitched land contour makes it possible to use the area under the new extension for a carport.

Such a room can be built quite large, perhaps 16 by 20 feet, the wider side being built along the present house wall. These are modular dimensions, which will simplify every stage of the project.

**Pier supports.** The room is supported on two or more masonry piers, supporting the far wall, and two similar piers adjacent to the existing house wall. No excavation is needed except to place footings for the piers. Heavy girder beams across the front and back piers support the floor joists, which can be placed at the level of your house floors. The room is built on the platform thus obtained.

Overhead, a shed roof is framed with rafters. There need be no alteration of the present roof lines, nor any major ripping out of the wall siding. Only one or two courses of shingles or clapboard need be taken out of the wall to install flashings at the new roof juncture, and some additional shingles where the new wall ties in at right angles to the original walls.

Elimination of the foundation wall represents a great saving in labor and materials. The floor joists for a suspended room will be of heavier stock than for other construction, either 3-by-8s if you can get them, or regular 2-by-10s, but the total cost differential is not very much. Inclusion of an exterior door with a stairway reaching to the yard will add quite a lot to the total, but of course will provide more convenience and utility for the recreation room.

**Open areaway preferred.** The area under the room may be left com-

Room addition adds to the appearance of a house, making it more impressive looking and providing interesting new lines. Where clapboard or shingle siding is used, try to align it with the original siding. Note access door for crawl space.

Inside view of a room extension has practical arrangement and attractive decorative styling. The suspended ceiling offers both acoustical and lighting qualities. The compass rose in the center of the floor is a ready-made insert which can be used in many designs.

Bring on the band! This music room is in harmony with the teen generation for gay, carefree evenings. Note the illuminated ceiling with individually controlled lighting for the panels.

Floor joists for room extension supported above grade on brick columns. Basement entranceway will be enlarged for head clearance when floor is completed. Doorway is opened to house through brick wall at back.

Room addition can also be constructed on a concrete slab. This extension is ready for wall framing. Roof rafters, supported on 4-by-4 posts, are insulated and covered with panels for maximum ceiling height. Floor will be built up on sleepers level with house floor at the door opening, which is framed and temporarily covered.

pletely open, or enclosed with a curtain wall for a crawl space. There is a widely held view that an open area like this always means that the room above will have a cold floor. That is not so. Adequate insulation and efficient heaters will assure complete comfort. In fact, there are many reasons to prefer an open, pier-supported room in contrast to some of the shortcomings of an enclosed crawl space.

In a crawl space, one of the chief problems is moisture rising from the soil, which condenses on the joists and floor, and soaks into the exposed insulation. The vapor also works into the rooms above, compounding the moisture problem. Another difficulty is clogging of the necessarily small air vents, causing dampness, unpleasant odors, and conditions favorable to invasion of insects.

An open space, to the contrary, is free of underside condensation. Adequate insulation, consisting of high-rated thermal blankets and thick insulation boards which completely cover the underside of the floor joists, will be fully effective.

**Pier spacing.** Standard pier spacing is 8 feet apart, on centers. However, this is modified by the strength of the beams that span the girders to support the floor joists. These must be not only strong enough to support the room extension but also sufficiently solid so the floors will not feel springy. A single-story room, 16 feet wide, of frame construction and lightweight exterior siding, such as aluminum, can be built with only two supporting columns at the far corners. Wood beams of 6-by-8-inch cross-section, or a 6-inch steel I-beam, will be needed for the floor supports. Placing an additional supporting pier or lally column between the corner piers will permit use of lighter cross beams.

**Placing the footings.** The footings must be dug deep enough so they are about 6 inches below the frost line, which is 3 to 4 feet in the northern areas.

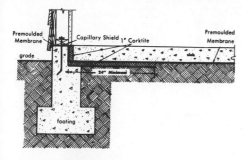

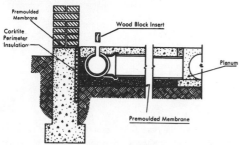

Drawing shows insulation of the concrete slab. Waterproof membrane completely isolates the structure from the soil and prevents migration of moisture into the slab. Perimeter insulation is essential for environmental conditioning.

Crawl space construction requires sealing of the open ground to prevent moisture condensation on the structural members, and also to keep area warm and dry. With proper vapor seal, no venting of the crawl space is required, and utility installations such as heating ducts and electrical cables are protected from rust.

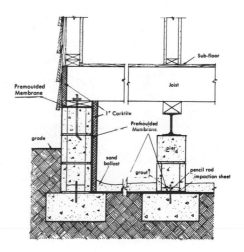

Size of the footing will depend on the kind of pier you will use. For concrete blocks, make the footing 16 by 16 inches, for brick 12 by 12 inches, and for poured concrete, 10 by 10 inches. The footing should be at least 12 inches thick.

Make the excavation large enough to give yourself room to set in the concrete forms, and to start the pier masonry. Box in the bottom of the excavation with a wood form, the width of the side boards being equal to the depth of the footing. Put in stakes to hold the form in level position. Before the footing concrete sets, insert a steel rod or pipe at the center to serve as reinforcement

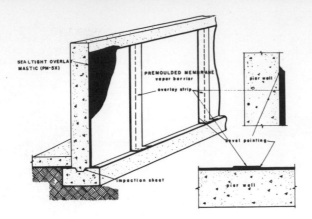

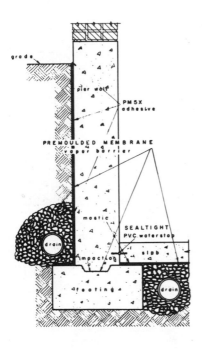

Basement walls and floor can be sealed against moisture from the ground only during course of construction, a detail that was omitted until recent years. Adequate drainage at the footing is required in any event. Drawing shows placement of premoulded membrane and the impaction sheet at wall-floor joint.

for the pier masonry. If you are going to use steel lally columns, anchor the column flange to bolts set deeply into the concrete.

After the footing concrete is well cured, erect the supporting columns. The essential detail here is that the columns be perfectly plumb, and that they be equal in height, that is, level. Check the masonry work frequently as you go with both spirit level and plumb bob. Whether of poured concrete, brick, or cement blocks, put anchoring bolts into the top for the girder. Steel lally columns are cut to measure and bolting plates attached at the time of purchase, or a standard length is used by installation of shim blocks to make up any differential in required length. A minor variation in level between the two corner piers is easily adjusted when the girder is put down.

For peak roof over room addition, rafters are angle-cut to fit against the center ridge board. Carpenter's square is calibrated to show the correct angles and length of beams.

Decking boards are nailed securely to the rafters. Make sure the boards are flat and uniformly aligned. Follow with a layer of felt paper and then the shingles.

Roof shingles should match the rest of the house in both color and design. Parallel courses must be kept straight and the specified overlap retained for each course. The critical point is the flashings where the new roof joins the original house wall.

**Termite shields.** Place metal termite shields between the piers and the girders. Install the floor joists, of 2-by-8 lumber, across the beams, 12 inches apart O.C. The front ends of the joists can extend beyond the beams by up to a foot if desired. Then lay a subfloor of ¾-inch commercial grade plywood over the joists, spacing the nails no more than 4 inches apart.

Floor insulation is put in from underneath, if there is enough height in the space below to work there; otherwise the insulation should go in from the top of the joists before the subfloor is laid. Use insulation batts of 4-inch thickness, the vapor side facing into the room. Underneath, across the joists, nail up 2-inch-thick rigid insulating boards to cover the entire underfloor area.

With the subfloor in place, the platform is completed. The walls now can be framed out with 4-by-4 corner posts and studs, as described in Chapter 12. Place double header plates across the top of the walls to support the roof rafters, and attach the near wall posts directly to the present house wall with masonry fasteners if necessary, caulking the joint both inside and outside.

**Roof is left intact.** The house wall need not be broken open to fit in the roof rafters. Rather, one or two courses of clapboard or shingle siding are removed, a 2-by-6 wood plate secured to the wall on which the rafters will be placed. Flashings will be placed under the lowest exposed siding course over the completed shed roof and the siding later replaced.

Put up the rafters at an adequate pitch according to the accepted practice in your area. The ceiling joists, like the rafters, rest on the double header across the front frame. Join the joists and the pitched rafters at that point with nails where they meet in the frame plate. These ceiling joists may be supported at the house side with a 2-by-6 carbel attached to the house wall, its top surface level with the wall frame header.

Aside from opening a door in the house wall leading into the room, the rest of this project proceeds with sheathing the wall frame, putting up the exterior siding, covering the roof, placing rain gutters and downspout, making electrical and heating connections, and putting up the wall panels, ceiling tiles, and the finished floor.

Here is the work schedule for building room addition:

1. Confirm approved building line of lot, by checking the survey.
2. Draw up and file plans.
3. Square the site for locating the support columns.
4. Excavate for footings. Place forms and pour concrete.
5. Build up masonry piers or columns to required height.
6. Span front and rear columns with anchored girders.
7. Lay in floor joists and sills.
8. Place insulation between joists, and nail on insulation board underneath.
9. Put down plywood subfloor. Place wall plates for frame.
10. Construct the wall framing. Install windows.
11. Attach rafter and ceiling joist support carbels to house wall.
12. Lay in rafters and cover with roof deck. Also the ceiling joists.
13. Make door opening from house, and hang door.
14. Rough in electric leads and boxes, and the heaters.
15. Insulate the walls and ceiling. Nail up outside sheathing.
16. Put up wall panels, ceiling tiles. Lay finished floor.
17. Finish outside walls with matching siding.

Door opening from house to room addition is cut by breaking through the plaster wall and cutting away the outside sheathing. When the intervening studs are removed, a double lintel is put across the opening before the new doorway is framed.

Outside of room built on slab is finished with insulating board used for sheathing. These panels are surely nailed to the framing studs and to the top and bottom plates.

Starter strips for the shingles are placed level on the walls, temporarily nailed for aligning the courses of shingles, and providing the required overlap for each course. Mineral fiber shingles come with holes for the nails.

**Cantilevered room.** A present den or bedroom that is too small for family use as a recreation room can be enlarged somewhat at moderate cost, thus avoiding a larger and more difficult construction. A cantilevered extension is built out from the present house wall supports, by breaking a wall opening the size of the present room and putting in new floor joists that are joined to the house framing. The maximum additional room depth that can be achieved in this manner, short of a major reinforcement of the house, would be about 6 feet. That would be enough to change the dimensions of an 8-by-12-foot room to one that is a usable 12 by 14 feet.

This project is limited in many cases by the nature of the house construction, as it means tearing out a section of exterior wall. This is not particularly difficult in a frame house, requiring only the installation of an adequate supporting member across the top of the wall opening, and supporting this header with doubled posts on each side in the wall. With a brick veneer house, however, a steel girder would have to be installed, with independent supporting posts or lally columns based on the foundation sill.

The cantilevered room is achieved by inserting floor beams through the opened side of the house, and linking these beams to the present floor joists. This can be done, only where you can reach the open joists in the basement to join them together, or by ripping up the present floor. The new joists are bolted securely to the old, and extra supports placed through the opening.

**Floor braced.** In some situations, the extended floor is additionally shored up with a diagonal brace which is supported on a beam placed at a lower level on the house wall. The need for a brace will depend on the distance that the room extends from the house wall, and the extent to which the new joists could be fastened to the old.

Elimination of a short section of its sill need not jeopardize the structural integrity of the house, if the new overhead lintels are of adequate strength and have been properly supported within the wall. In any such major house operation, it is necessary to make sure that any changes will not cause shifting or new settling. This is a job that should be done only with the advice of an architect, and the plans scrupulously followed. But the project does offer at least another method of obtaining a recreation room within the limited living space.

**Using a garage deck.** In two-story houses, decks on garage roofs are, strangely, pretty much in limbo. People just don't use them much, if at all. When enclosed as an all-weather room, however, they make a fine den or study. Such a room, if built over the entire garage roof, would be quite large, with enough space to possibly include an extra bathroom, or at least some storage closets, in your plans.

A frequently observed drawback to this arrangement, though, occurs when the garage deck adjoins one or more upper floor bedrooms, making direct access to the garage room problematical. One way around this, where space allows, is to partition off a narrow part of one bedroom to make a corridor passageway to the roof room. Another way is to take over a closet in the bedroom, switching the door to face into the house hall, and make the closet part of a passageway to the new den. A substitute wardrobe can be built into the bedroom. Presumably, there already is a door from the bedroom to the garage deck, but its location may not be correctly placed for the new room entrance.

**Reverse-pitch roof.** Enclosing the upper deck of the garage also raises the roof, literally, by threatening to alter the basic roof line for the entire house. Here's a solution that has worked well in other homes. Pitch the new roof from the far end of the room down toward the back, instead of the conventional shed roof slope, and where the roof lines meet at the present house line, they form a valley that can be flashed into a drain.

If you can overcome these basic difficulties, the actual building of the room will follow quite closely that for converting an attached garage.

Remember that a roof over a garage is practically out in the open, so pay particular attention to insulating the new floor, as well as the walls and ceiling, provide for adequate heating and cooling, and use insulating glass for the windows.

# CHAPTER NINE

# INSULATING YOUR ROOM

Two KINDS of insulation, thermal plus a vapor barrier, combine to keep your room comfortably warm or cool, as the season demands, and to protect it from the ravages of trapped condensation. Control of heat loss cuts fuel bills, eases the load on the furnace, minimizes drafts, and keeps the room temperature at a uniform level.

Adequate insulation thus is vital to the success of your recreation room project. How much insulation to use is best answered by, "the more the better." However, there are priorities; some places require more insulation than others. Insulation is rated by "R" values—the higher the number, the more effective it is, though many brands still are specified by inches of thickness of material. Generally, the recommended quality requirement for a ceiling is R-19, or 6-inch thickness, for walls R-13, or 4 inches, and the same for floors over unheated spaces.

**Vapor barrier important.** Humidity is fine in the home. It helps to ease breathing for people with respiratory difficulties. It is also good for furniture, as it keeps glued joints from coming apart.

But humidity can play havoc with the house itself. That happens when the vapor-laden warm air passes through the wall and ceiling plaster, seeking a cooler surface on which to unload its moisture by condensation. In enclosed places, such as inside the walls, in crawl spaces, between floors, and inside attics, this condensate causes rotted beams, mildew, soaked insulation fibers, blistered and peeling paint on exterior walls, cracked and loosened ceiling plaster, termites, and in the case of basements, nasty damp odors.

The amount of water in the home atmosphere is dramatically demonstrated by an electric dehumidifier, which in a single day can extract 5 gallons of water from the air. With no vapor barrier, a wall of 1,000 square feet might allow 2½ gallons of water to pass through in 24 hours. Most of this vapor, indeed, will pass through to the outside air, but enough might remain inside the wall space to blister the paint right off. The exterior siding, rot the wall lumber, or soak the insulation.

Air vents in the curtain walls of crawl spaces are intended to exhaust the vapor before it condenses on floor joists under the room. In attics, open louvers exhaust humid air which otherwise would condense on the rafters and the underside of the roof deck, starting rot.

However well every other part of the project has been handled, it is the insulation that will make the difference for complete comfort and fuel economy for your new recreation room. A fully foil-enclosed insulation blanket need be only half as thick to provide the same insulating value.

Insulation comes in widths to fit snugly between studs and joists spaced 12, 16, or 24 inches on centers. The paper batts or blankets have tough flanges which are bent over the wood framing and fastened with staples. Hammer-type stapling gun speeds the work.

Another situation is moisture migration from the ground soil into a structure, either in the form of vapor, or by capillary action caused by variations in atmospheric pressure. This is the reason for using a membrane sheeting spread over open soil areas of crawl spaces and under poured concrete slabs.

**Types of insulation materials.** The insulation blanket consists of fibrous material enclosed in specially treated heavy kraft paper covering. The fibrous material may be fiberglass, mineral wool (the fine fibers obtained by spinning molten limestone rock, blast furnace slag, or glass), balsam wood fibers, and other material.

One surface of the insulating blanket or batt is impregnated with water-proofing material to form a skin which is the vapor barrier. The vapor barrier side is always installed facing toward the interior, or warm side, of the house. You can remember this best by keeping in mind that the vapor barrier's purpose is to prevent vapor passage that would condense in the insulation material.

When measuring for required length, add enough to allow foldover at top and bottom to completely enclose the space. Always apply the blanket with the vapor side facing into the room.

Short blanket, leaving open space, defeats the purpose of the installation. The essential point is that the room is completely sealed for both thermal and moisture control. Pack any open spaces with loose fiber wool, and cover with plastic membrane sheeting.

The blankets come in long rolls, to be cut as necessary on the job. This permits putting in a long run of insulation with a minimum of butted joints. Batts are similar, but come precut to standard length, usually 4 and 8 feet. Both kinds are supplied in 11, 15, 19 and 23-inch widths that fit between studs and floor joists that are 12, 16, 20, and 24 inches on centers. The sides have flanges for easy stapling to the framing members.

At top and bottom of a stud enclosure, the blanket is folded over the framing and tacked down. To do this, remove about 2 inches of the insulation wool. Save this material for use in packing small spaces.

Ceiling of room addition receives maximum insulating priority. Here the insulation batts are fitted tightly between the joist bridging. Six-inch thickness is recommended.

In attic, insulation is carried to every corner and space within the enclosed area, trimmed to fit if necessary and tightly stapled in place.

The insulation has a kraft paper binding, some with a metal foil facing, others completely foil-enclosed. There also is a pouring wool for filling spaces which cannot be covered with an insulation batt.

Two other insulation materials are important for the recreation room project. One is a thin plastic membrane for use under poured concrete slabs and in crawl spaces. The other is a rigid fiberglass and asbestos board for perimeter insulation around the footing of floor slabs and the inside walls of crawl spaces. The board comes in thicknesses from 1 to 2 inches, and in various panel sizes up to 2-by-4. Similar thick fiberglass or cork boards are used for roof insulation.

Special-purpose insulation materials include molded shapes for heating and water lines, and also sound-control types.

**Installation rules.** When installing the blankets, think of each section of the house framing as an individual unit to be insulated. For example, the space between two wall studs, ending at the floor and ceiling, will require an insulating mat completely sealing the whole surface, with an air space between the mat and the outside wall sheathing. Do each such section thoroughly, one at a time, so that you know it will serve its purpose well.

For narrow sections around door or window frames, cut the blanket to required width for packing into place. Allow extra width on vapor side of paper for stapling flange.

At heater ducts, around air conditioners, and all other obstructions that prevent use of regular lengths of the batting, pack fibers tightly into the narrow spaces, using the material cut from the ends of regular runs.

Completed wall has continuous vapor barrier even over the small wall sections that were individually packed. Use enough staples to hold the batts firmly.

In some places spaces may be filled more easily by pouring insulation pellets, but a separate vapor barrier will be needed. In the case of a space above an attic room, the pellets are packed above the regular batting, which has a vapor barrier and was stapled to the joists from below.

```
    BTUH HEAT LOSS COMPARISON WITH MINIMUM AND
        RECOMMENDED AMOUNTS OF INSULATION


                RANCH TYPE HOUSE

        NET WALL           AREA    1218 SQ.FT.
        WINDOW AND FLOOR   AREA     217 SQ.FT.
        CEILING-FLOOR      AREA    1383 SQ.FT.

        INDOOR-OUTDOOR DESIGN TEMP. 75F

        SINGLE GLAZED WINDOWS
        NON-WEATHERSTRIPPED
```

MINIMUM INSULATION

* HEAT LOSS 82,000 BTUH
* R-7 CEILING INSULATION
* NO SIDEWALL OR FLOOR
      INSULATION
* EST. HEAT COST - $500

RECOMMENDED INSULATION

* HEAT LOSS 44,600 BTUH
* R-19 CEILING INSULATION
* R-13 WALL INSULATION
* R-13 FLOOR INSULATION
* EST. HEAT COST - $272

Chart shows extent of heat loss in ranch house of 1218 square feet with minimum insulation, and one with recommended insulation. The difference of cost for heating in a single year is 45% in this example. The differential will vary according to location and type of fuel.

**Where the insulation goes.** Each kind of room project requires its own approach to insulation procedures. In basement rooms whose foundation walls are below grade, vinyl asbestos floor tiles and the mastic adhesive form an adequate vapor seal. Though the floor will be cooler than the other room surfaces in the summer, condensation is usually minimal because of the tendency of warm, vapor-laden air to rise.

The practicality of placing thermal insulation with a vapor barrier skin between wall studs in below-grade basements is highly questionable because of the probability that vapor absorbed through the foundation would condense inside the insulation blanket. However, if it is decided that the basement requires such insulation for added warmth, or to protect the wall paneling, an effective measure is to seal the walls with an asphaltum paint.

**Attic insulation.** Thorough insulation together with proper ventilation are essential in attic rooms, for both summer and winter comfort, and to safeguard the structure of the home against trapped condensate. In the room, insulation blankets are fitted between studs at the knee walls, end walls, the sloped ceilings, and between joists across the top ceiling. Dormers particularly must be fully insulated at the sides, front, and the ceiling covering, because of their exposed position which provide a cooler condensing surface.

Make sure that there are adequate louvered vents at opposite ends under the roof peak and above the new dropped ceiling. Also the enclosed spaces in the peaks above window dormers must have some provision for venting.

**Rooms on concrete slabs.** Unless constructed with proper attention to insulation and vapor barrier requirements, rooms built on concrete slabs are particularly vulnerable to excessive heat loss and condensation problems. But these conditions must be provided for at the time of construction, and can rarely be corrected in the completed room.

The fundamental requirements are an effective vapor barrier under the slab (placed before the concrete is poured) and a perimeter insulation of rigid boards. For a slab membrane, use heavy-grade coated roofing felt, all joints of which are lapped at least 3 inches. A deficiency here is the possibility that the felt will be torn or penetrated by the stones as the concrete is poured, making the barrier ineffective. In current practice, builders use a premolded plastic membrane which is completely waterproof and has maximum resistance to damage.

**Perimeter insulation.** For heat protection, insulation boards are placed all around inside the footing. The slab concrete is poured against it and thus the floor is separated from its outside wall. Also, the rigid insulating boards are fitted around the outside perimeter of the foundation. An existing concrete floor in a converted porch room should at least have the masonry footing protected around the outside with insulating board. This will require digging a trench a couple of feet deep so that the boards can be glued against the walls, with metal flashing fitted under the wall siding and over these boards to prevent water entry.

Rooms on concrete slabs are insulated inside, as explained below, with blankets between the floor sleepers, in walls and ceiling under the roof.

**Crawl spaces.** Crawl spaces usually are 18 to 24 inches in height, have

Workmen laying in a premoulded vapor seal membrane before pouring concrete slab. Edges of the membrane are joined with special cement.

wood floor joists supported on masonry walls or posts. Proper insulation of the exposed floor joists underneath is essential for warmth, and to protect the joists from deterioration caused by vapor condensation in their highly vulnerable location.

Control of moisture is a first step, and involves blocking vapor rising from the soil. The excavated soil should receive a layer of sand ballast. This is covered with a heavy waterproof roofing felt, lapped 6 inches along edges, and bent up 6 inches along the foundation walls. A more effective vapor protection is afforded by premolded membrane, like Sealtight, composed of asphalt impregnated mineral fibers and mineral aggregates. A single sheet of Mylar, a plastic, is even better.

Line the foundation walls with rigid fiberglass insulating boards, secured to the masonry with a special adhesive. Remember that such crawl spaces must have at least four louvered vents, kept open all year for air movement.

Next, the exposed floor joists are insulated. This may be done with (1) rigid insulation board 1 inch thick nailed across the bottom of the joists, and the open spaces packed with loose pouring wool or Vermiculate; (2) insulation blankets squeezed high up between the joists, and the blanket flanges tacked to the sides; or (3) blankets 3 inches thick stapled through the flanges to the underside of the joists and supported by galvanized mesh to prevent sagging. The vapor barrier of the blanket faces the warm side, into the room.

Walls and ceiling of the room are insulated with 4- and 6-inch batts. For superior heat retention, install an additional layer of rigid roof insulation like Pittsburgh Plate Glass Company's Foamglas boards, in 1- or 1½-inch thickness, over the roof deck.

105

Insulation fibers blown into house wall through holes drilled in the sliding, or other means of access. This method is more costly than would have been the case if adequate insulation was installed at time house was built.

**Converted garage room.** Good insulation of the concrete garage floor is essential for comfort. The spaces between the floor sleepers can be packed with pouring wool, or insulated with 6-inch blankets, stapled to the side flanges and with vapor side facing into the room. The exterior walls receive 4-inch insulation blankets between studs, and the ceiling joists are packed with 6-inch blankets, unless the room is under another one on the next floor, in which case 4-inch blankets will do for sound-deadening as well as a heat barrier.

**Applying batts or blankets.** Batts come in flat packages, cut to 4- or 8-foot length; blankets are in rolls and are cut as needed on the job. Both have side flanges for stapling to the studs or joists. One side of the blanket is marked as the vapor barrier. The foil wrapped type will have provision for a vapor barrier on one side, clearly indicated.

When handling, be careful to avoid tearing the paper covers, particularly the vapor barrier; any opening or puncture defeats the purpose of the seal. Basic rules include the following: when joining two lengths of blanket, butt the ends tightly together. When starting a run at a joist, carry the insulation over the top of the wall plate, and tack the free end to the plate for complete closure.

At wall studs, the blanket is fitted between two studs, pressed in slightly so the side flanges line up with the front edges of the studs. Remove some fiber packing from the top end, so the envelope paper can be folded down to form a flange for stapling in place. Repeat at the bottom. Thus, the entire wall unit of the two studs and insulation blanket is fully and tightly sealed.

When encountering electric boxes or water pipes within the stud space, press the insulation behind the pipe, if possible, otherwise pass the blanket in front of it. At any place where the insulation must be cut open, to clear an electric switch, for instance, make the cutout opening smaller than needed, so the insulation will pack in tightly against the obstruction.

**For attic insulation,** cover the knee walls, sloped ceiling, and top ceiling with separate lengths of blanket. While a continuous run can be done with a single length up one knee wall, and across the ceiling to the other side, without a joint, this method may result in buckling the blanket.

Best way is to do the short knee wall, then bring a length of blanket down from the ceiling joint of the sloped ceiling section to butt against the knee wall strip, the vapor barrier overlapping it. Finally, fit the ceiling batt with attention to the side joints.

If any stud or joist spacing is too far apart for the blanket flanges to reach across, nail up furring strips along the side of the joist to fill the gap. Do not try to stretch the flanges farther than they are intended to go.

Always difficult to do, but critical for insulating purposes, are the rough frames around doors and windows, as there is a space between the framing members and the door jambs. Save the fibers removed from the ends of the blankets for packing into the door and window frames.

These are narrow spaces and do not offer much surface area for vapor penetration. However, because they are alongside windows, which are likely to be cooler than the rest of the room and thus more vulnerable to condensation, you can make your own vapor barrier from heavy-grade polyethylene sheeting, cut into strips and stapled over the packed insulating wool.

In addition to insulation, windows should be properly weatherstripped to reduce air leaks. Good quality wood windows now come completely weatherstripped from the factory, but any that are not should be grooved and fitted with interlocking metal splines for sealed closure. In some cases, storm sash also will be needed, particularly on windows facing prevailing winds. Best of all is the double pane insulated window. Though heavy and quite expensive, they do the job that can be achieved in no other way, permit use of large glass areas in the room, and eliminate need for storm windows.

Always wear gloves and tight-fitting clothes when working with fiberglass insulation. Otherwise glass fibers will get on your body and badly irritate your skin.

# CHAPTER TEN

# ELECTRIC WIRING, HEATERS AND FIREPLACES

MAKE UP your mind, right from the start, that your electric wiring will be top notch, of quality materials, planned to adequately supply your electrical needs, and installed to conform with local regulations and the Electrical Code. Careless or amateurish wiring can be troublesome and dangerous. A proper electric installation, on the other hand, puts wonderful resources at your command for luxurious comfort with air conditioners, instant heaters, dehumidifiers, power tools, and other equipment, all functioning dependably and safely without the slightest concern on your part.

It is certainly advisable to have the entire electrical work done by a licensed electrician. Many homeowners, however, are perfectly capable through experience and innate mechanical aptitude to do at least part of this work in good order. In any event, it's worth while to understand what comprises the domestic electric service, the kinds of circuits, their load capacities and limits, and the basic wiring techniques. Wiring is much easier today than it was just a few years ago because the new plastic wire coating that has replaced the bulky rubber insulation is slimmer, easier to bend and strip. Thus, the heavier No. 12 wire can be used with 20-ampere fuses to handle a larger appliance load, in place of the old No. 14 wire. Also, many of the wiring devices have been improved, including easier-to-install brackets and clamp-type conduit couplings.

**Wiring circuits.** The electric service that comes into your house is divided at the fuse box into a number of branch circuits for distributing the current to different parts of the house. Each circuit has its own fuse, rated in amperes according to the load-carrying capacity of that circuit.

The capacity of a circuit depends mostly on the size of its wire. A circuit with No. 12 wire will have a 20-ampere fuse, with a current-carrying capacity of up to 2,400 watts. If current beyond that wattage is drawn, the wire will overheat and blow the fuse. Such 20-ampere "general purpose" circuits are for lights and small appliances like a vacuum cleaner, television, and toaster.

Two such circuits in the recreation room should supply the current needed for ordinary use, unless you have a high-wattage electric space heater, which will need its own circuit. You can compute the circuit needs by adding up the wattage ratings for different electrical appliances, given in the accompanying chart, that would be used in the family room.

Good lighting makes all the difference in the enjoyment of a family room, whether for games, reading the paper, or just a bright attractive appearance.

One fundamental requirement of the Electrical Code is that the lighting outlets of any room be divided between two or more circuits so that in the event a fuse blows, the room won't be thrown into complete darkness.

Let's see what would happen in a room with a single circuit. Suppose the lighting totals 400 watts, the guests are listening to the stereo record player (300 watts), the coffee maker is perking away (600 watts), and the toaster is on (1100 watts)—a total of 2,400 watts, just about the maximum. Someone switches on the blender to mix some cocktails, and the extra 250 watts overloads the circuit. Suddenly, the room is in complete darkness—the fuse has blown.

Your guests are discomfited and you have to bungle about in the dark to replace the fuse. If there were no fuse, the wires would heat up enough to cause a fire, very likely behind the walls where it would get a good start before you would know about it.

With two branch circuits properly distributed in the room, current drawn by the appliances would be at least partially divided between them, so there would be no overload. But in the event that one fuse blows for any reason, the other circuit would continue and the room would still be lighted.

There's still another factor to recognize. That is the voltage drop which accompanies the draw on wattage. Motors operating on less than their rated voltage not only do not function efficiently, but also tend to burn out. Thus an air conditioner motor would labor excessively and deliver less cool air if the circuit to which it is connected has a heavy current drain from lamps and other appliances.

109

## WATTAGE RATINGS

| | |
|---|---|
| Vacuum cleaner | 400 |
| Television | 300 |
| Stereo hi-fi | 300 |
| Coffee maker | 600 |
| Blender | 250 |
| Refrigerator | 150 |
| Food mixer | 150 |
| Large grill or rotisserie | 1300 |
| Toaster | 1100 |
| Ironer | 1600 |
| Hand iron | 1000 |
| Sump pump | 300 |
| Electric space heater | 1000 to 3000 |
| Air conditioner | 1200 to 2000 |

Good electric wiring practice requires that major appliances, like air conditioners and space heaters, be supplied by individual circuits. With a properly planned wiring layout, you can be free of the annoyance of blown fuses, and your appliances will function economically and at peak efficiency.

Even plants blossom indoors when there's plentiful light, adding their brilliant colors to your room decoration. Ceiling spots make an effective addition to your lighting scheme, but don't neglect the regular table lamps for homey color.

Easiest fixture to install in a tiled ceiling is one made especially for the purpose. The fixture is simply inserted in place of a standard 12-by-12 tile at the time of ceiling installation. The fixture comes completely prewired with its own junction box.

One thing more: if your home has a 220-volt electric service, it is better to use appliances designed for 220 rather than 110-volt current, and the wiring plan for your room should include three-wire cables as explained later.

**Wiring plan.** Draw up a definite plan for the electric installations in the room. The room should have an outlet at least every 12 feet of wall space around the room, but be sure to include outlets at additional locations where they will be needed so there will be no need to use long extension cords to reach different electric units. Include an outlet specifically at the location of any pole lamps, table lamps, TV, record player, wall clock, fireplace (if it will burn electric logs), at the serving buffet for a toaster, blender, or coffee percolator. A diagram should show the distribution of wires from the different circuit cables and the wall switches.

Your workshop needs its own circuits, so that motors on power tools do not put an excess current drain on a line supplying your recreation room, or dim the house lights. Laundry appliances, particularly an electric dryer, require heavier electric wire and a circuit with 30-ampere fuse.

**Roughing in.** Actual wiring can be done efficiently only by following a diagram showing how all connections are to be made. Installation starts with "roughing in" the metal utility boxes for outlets, switches, and ceiling fixtures. These boxes are securely fastened to the framing studs with nails. All junction and outlet boxes must be so located that they are always accessible by removing the covers. The cables are brought into the room from the location of the main fuse box, but these cables are not hooked into the power lines until all the connections are completed. Thus you can work with the wires in complete safety.

**Types of Cables.** Cables come in several types. BX cables are insulated wires in a protective spiral metal sheath, which is sufficiently flexible to be carried inside walls and around obstructions. Nonmetallic cables have a heavy

Another type of light fixture particularly suitable for recreation rooms is the 25-inch-square Imperialite made by Emerson Electric Co. The fixture has a walnut frame and decorative plastic grill that diffuses the light.

One of the newest forms of decorating with light is with luminous wall panels. Fluorescent tubes, concealed behind sheets of plastic or other diffusing materials, provide a cheery background that extends the range and scope of the room. The panels are ideal for concealing unsightly architectural elements in a room improvement project. Sliding panels give access to the rear for changing the lamps. The use of varied-colored lamp tubes will increase the interest, and a group of light switches can control the color scheme at will.

Source of the house electricity is the circuit box, where the main feeder line branches off into circuits, to serve different rooms and appliances. Each circuit starts at one of the terminal blocks shown in the metal box.

plastic covering, approved in most localities. Thin-wall conduit is used with separate insulated wire drawn through after the entire conduit is installed. Several pairs of wires are contained in a single conduit.

The cables have either two or three current-carrying wires, plus an extra grounding wire. BX cables may be used without the extra wire, as the metal sheath can serve for grounding, but it still is better to have the separate wire because it provides an assured grounding contact and is easier to make the connections.

Two-wire cables are used for regular lighting and appliance circuits. Three-wire cables bring in two circuits in a single cable, or 220 volts with a single white neutral wire. Also, three-wire cables are needed for connecting three-way light switches at stairways.

**Stripping wires.** The photographs show how a stripping plier skins wire insulation, how connections are made to receptacles and fixture terminals, how knockouts provide entries in metal boxes, and how cable wires are spliced and taped inside junction boxes. Rectangular boxes with special mounting brackets for attaching to wall studs are used for outlets and wall switches, octagonal boxes for ceiling fixtures are mounted with adjustable bar hangers long enough to reach across joists or studs. Where two or more wall switches are placed together, a gang box for switches is made up by combining the required number of special steel boxes that have removable sides.

Good wiring technique requires that:

1. Only enough insulation be stripped to leave about ½″ of bare wire for terminal connection.

2. Only one wire under each screw.

113

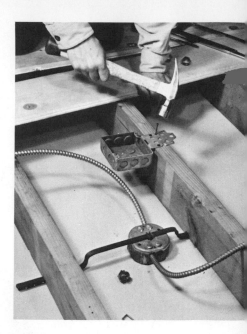

Junction boxes usually are square or octagonal, with knockout openings at the side. Each box has one or another type of attachment bracket, which is securely nailed to the wall framing.

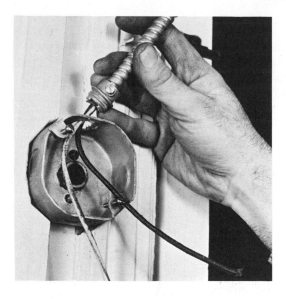

Every cable entry into a junction, switch, or receptacle box is securely locked in place with special cable connectors, in which a lock nut is turned on from inside the box.

3. Spliced wires are intertwined and joined by wire nuts, and splices made only in junction boxes.

4. Cables are secured at every electric box with connectors or clamps.

5. BX cables receive a protective plastic bushing at every box connection.

6. The grounding wire in nonmetallic cables is attached to every electric box or to polarized outlet terminals.

7. All concealed wiring that goes behind walls, under the floor, or between ceiling joists, always is with Code-approved cables strapped every 4½ feet and near all connector boxes. Exposed cable is strapped every 3 feet.

Wire stripper is an essential tool that will speed the electrical installation. Closure is adjusted for the different wire gauges. Cutters slice the insulation at neat bevel. Cut the stripped wire to required length.

Continuity of grounding wire is important. When three-prong safety receptacles are used, connect the ground terminal to the third wire of the cable, if it has one; otherwise use a jumper wire attached to one of the metal box screws when using BX cables or metal conduit.

**Making connections.** When all outlet switch boxes in a room are fastened in place, run the cable wires to them. The cable can run through holes drilled in the studs, or along notches cut in front of the studs to recess the cable flush with the stud face. In the ceiling, run the cable between the joists.

In the basement, it will be simple enough to run the cable from your service box to the room location. This will be more difficult for an attic room and rooms built onto the house, as the cables will have to be fished up behind the walls for concealed installation. In a one-story house, you can do this easily enough by drilling holes in the floor and ceiling at a back corner of a closet, running the cable up from the basement inside the closet. The cables then are continued between the joists to the attic room, or down through the ceiling again to the location of the new room. Where the room is an entirely new addition with a slab floor, you may find that the best way is to fish the cable from the basement up into the frame of the door leading to the room, and along the ceiling to the various outlets.

Fishing the cable is done with a wire "snake," and can take quite a while to accomplish, but your patience will be well rewarded when you feel the snake pass beyond any obstacles. Then the cable end is securely attached to the hook at the end of the snake, bound with electrical tape, and drawn up to the attic.

**Wiring of switches** can be quite complex, so make a diagram for each switch to help avoid time-consuming errors. Various switch arrangements are shown in the accompanying diagrams. Also shown is the method for controlling lights from two or three locations. This is important at stairways, and also where rooms have more than one entrance, so that lights can be turned on when entering from any door, and turned off when leaving at another door.

Not until all outlet and switch connections have been made are the cables hooked into the circuit box, and the lines fused. Watch to see whether any fuse blows, as this would show some fault in the installation or a defective device which must be immediately tracked down. A simple tester with a neon-type lamp will help locate the source of the trouble.

**Tracing a short.** Disconnect all lamps on that circuit by pulling the plugs, and turn off any wall switches that had been on. Screw a 100-watt light bulb into the fuse socket. If the bulb lights, that indicates a short in the circuit which can be traced with the neon tester. If the bulb does not light, then one of the lamps or appliances in the circuit is shorted.

Try each lamp in the room, one at a time. If plugging in a lamp causes the bulb at the circuit box to light, but the lamp does not, then it is the cause of the short. Remove it, and try the other lights on the circuit, replacing the fuse in the circuit box.

When the electric installation is checked out, a few additional details remain to be done before tackling the wall panels.

**Low-voltage wiring.** If the room is to have a space heater, or a zone control on your hot water heating system, install the necessary thermostat and its wiring. Other items that should be installed at this time are telephone, annunciator, intercom, and perhaps burglar alarm wiring.

When you do this, it might be a good idea to provide for future needs by running a cable with extra low-voltage wires from a central station in the new room into the basement or other location where the wires can be reached when needed. An example of such use would be connecting a pair of speakers from your hi-fi set in the workshop, laundry, or other room.

Location of the thermostat needs a little thought to make it fully effective for your comfort. It should not be placed near a TV or a record player that gives off heat, as this would cause the thermostat to shut off because this area was warm while the rest of the room might be quite chilly. Nor should it be near drafts from an open doorway, in an inside corner of the room, or where it would be affected by direct rays of the sun. Best location is several feet from an outside doorway or exterior wall, and at eye-level height.

**Polarized grounding plugs.** The extra grounding wire in your cables can be a lifesaver, taking the shock hazard out of handling an appliance that has become shorted. But this protection works only if the receptacle is connected to the ground wire, and the appliance or tool has a polarized three-prong plug, the third being for grounding contact. At the small extra cost, it would be wise to install the safety grounding receptacles, particularly at the serving buffet and in the workshop.

**Using conduit.** Thin-wall conduit of galvanized steel has the advantages of better fire safety, assured continuous ground, and protection against accidental damage to the wires by nails and other causes.

The conduit used for home work is ½ or ¾ inch in diameter, and comes in easily handled 10-foot lengths. Lengths can be cut with a hacksaw or wheel pipe cutter and joined to each other or locked into junction boxes with clamping type connectors.

The burr on the inside of the conduit must be removed with a reamer to allow free passage of wires that will be inserted, and to prevent the sharp edges from cutting into the wire insulation.

Only four bends of up to 90 degrees each in any run of conduit between boxes are allowed by the code. The conduit installation is completed before the wires are drawn through. A fish tape, or "snake," which is available in 50-foot and 100-foot lengths, is used to help pull the wires. The wires that will be needed are tied into a bundle and pulled through at one time, all tied to the fish tape.

Conduit is always joined into a metal electric box, locked in with connectors. When both conduit and BX cables are used in combination for an installation, the splice must be made inside a junction box, to which both the BX and conduit are securely fastened with connectors.

**Sizes of conduit.** Be careful to select conduit of sufficient diameter to provide for all expected—and even unexpected—needs. Obviously it will be very frustrating and expensive to find after the conduit is in place that it isn't large enough to receive all the wires you need for the recreation room, and the extras that come up, like a feeder line for a sump pump. Half-inch conduit carries four No. 14 wires or three No. 12 wires. Three-quarter-inch conduit carries four No. 10 or No. 12 wires.

Following are the current-carrying capacities of circuit wires in conduit or cable:

| Wire Size | Amperes |
|-----------|---------|
| No. 14 | 15 |
| No. 12 | 20 |
| No. 10 | 30 |

**SPACE HEATING.** The serviceability and pleasure obtained from your new room will depend to large measure on how comfortably it is heated. A room extension that is not an integral part of the structure tends to be colder than the rest of the house, even though it may be well-built and fully insulated, possibly because it is more exposed and lacks heat retention to the same degree. Basement and attic rooms, to the contrary, are easily heated, if the house equipment is in good order.

In nearly all homes, the present heating system has a sufficient margin of BTU capacity to take care of an additional room, but it is problematical

Baseboard heaters are most effective for room extensions. Heaters are easily installed, attached directly to the wall panels and are quite attractive in appearance. This is an electric heater.

Cutaway view shows the arrangement of fins in baseboard convector. The Slant/Fin unit is used with hot water or steam systems.

whether to use the present system or rely on the alternative of a separate space heater. Installing a hookup to the central heater may involve considerable difficulty. In contrast, most of the new space heaters are extremely simple to install, with some models requiring no plumbing connection.

Procedures for connections to a present heating system vary in each instance according to type of heating, location of room, and access to a duct or tubing.

**Forced hot-air heater.** In a house with forced hot-air heater, a new room backing on another with the duct in a mutual wall, can receive the hot-air circulation by means of a new register cut into the same wall duct. An attic room in a one-story house may be supplied with the duct extended through a closet on the floor below.

Fan-forced heat from newer unit made by Emerson Electric Co. is available in capacity ranges from 1,500 to 4,000 watts. Design will blend with any room decor.

Heating connections may involve cutting and threading of pipes. Shown here is a union coupling used to rejoin cut-away sections after inserting a Tee fitting for the new connection.

Hot-water radiators are connected to an existing hot-water heating line by means of two tees. One is always a standard tee, the other is always a special tee made for heating lines. Pipe of a type and size similar to that used with the other radiators may be used to connect each end of a new radiator to its pair of tees.

**Steam connection.** When the existing radiators are connected by a single pipe to the main steam line, new radiators are also connected by a single pipe to the same line. When existing radiators are connected by two pipes, one to the main steam line and the other to the return main, the new radiator(s) must be connected the same way. Radiators may be positioned wherever desired as long as they are above the main(s) and as long as the connecting pipe(s) run continuously downhill. A slight upturn produces a "valley" which collects water and causes steam blockage and noise.

Basement rooms usually present no heating problems, located as they are near the furnace room with the heating pipes or ducts passing right through the room. But even here supplementary provisions for heating are needed, for one thing to assure dryness of the basement.

A useful adjunct to basement heating is an inexpensive little gadget called Thermo-fins. These are interlocking aluminum fins that are clamped over hot-water or steam pipes. The fins radiate heat from the pipes, the number of fins in the row determining the amount of heat radiated. Six feet of the fins on a pipe will heat an average-sized basement room.

**Baseboard radiation.** Separate and independent electric baseboard hot-water heaters seem the ideal way to provide quick, constant heating comfort to a well-insulated recreation room. The units are completely quiet, automatically controlled by an individual thermostat, quite handsome in appearance.

Installation is exceedingly simple, as the unit comes completely assembled and is merely attached to the wall panels with a special nailing tool or screws.

Most models for permanent installation operate on 240 volts, so they would not be any value to the home with only a 120-volt system. However, there is a portable heater that operates on 120 volts.

Wattage range of these heaters is from 300 up to 1,380, and BTU hour output from 1,050 for the smallest unit to 4,700. The manufacturer of these heaters, Intertherm Company, 3800 Park Avenue, St. Louis, Missouri, 63110, offers to supply without charge an engineered heater layout and an estimate of heating costs, using their electric units. The method of computation is given on the basis of local electric rates, which you can obtain by phoning your utility company. Electricity rates run from 2 to 5 cents per 1,000 watts per hour, depending on the region. But be wary of accepting an estimate based on maximum 68-degree temperature, which most people find uncomfortable. The cost of heating to 70 or 72 degrees will be considerably more.

**Cost estimate.** Figuring that a 1,000-watt heater is "on" only 25 percent of the time, this gives a total of 180 hours a month. Thus, at 2 cents average rate for a kilowatt hour, the month's charge for 180 kilowatt hours, multiplied by 2 cents, is $3.60 a month per heater. In the extremely cold months, like January, if the heater is on for half the time each day, the total cost for current would be $7.20, by this computation. The "On" time is an important factor, as the thermostat shuts o' the heater the instant that the desired temperature is reached, though the circulating hot water in the unit continues to maintain warmth, acccording to the manufacturer. An average-sized family room might require two or more of the 1,000 watt units.

A baseboard convector heater with models for either 120 or 240 volts is manufactured by Emerson Electric Company of St. Louis, Missouri, 63136. These are easily installed in a three-step operation, and are designed to be recessed between studs 16 inches O.C. Both units can be connected to No. 14 wire feeds. The 120-volt heater ranges from 450 to 2,000 watts, while the 240-volt model is from 525 to 1,400 watts.

Emerson makes a basement model with fan-forced heat for instant, evenly distributed warmth without drafts or cold spots, requires 240-volt current, and pulls 1,500 to 4,000 watts. A similar fan-type model is rectangular in shape for wall mounting between studs at any desired height.

**Basement heating.** Most basements are fairly well heated by the furnace, and the steam pipes, hot-water tubing, or warm-air ducts that pass along the basement ceiling joists. Much depends, of course, on both the location of these heating lines and whether they are insulated. There are several simple and inexpensive courses you can take to assure that a basement recreation room and other basement areas will be comfortably warm in all weather.

A slight dampness in the basement will contribute to a chilly feeling. However, when the walls are framed out and paneled, and the floor surfaced, there is an improvement because the concrete is insulated from condensation. Additional steps can include cutting several openings for registers in warm-air ducts, or placing rows of sheet-metal fins along steam and hot-water lines for greater heat convection.

If these are not sufficient, or the heating lines do not extend to the far reaches of the basement, you can install an additional radiator on a circulating hot-water system. Such a radiator should be mounted high on the ceiling to assure better water flow.

Steam radiators, however, cannot be placed below the main feed line. You will get good results, however, by removing the insulation packing around the steam feeder pipes. There will be very little loss of total heat by removal of the pipe covering, as warming the basement does much to heat up the entire house, and the production of steam is controlled by the upstairs thermostat.

Where the foregoing suggestions do not produce adequate results, the addition of one or two electric radiant heaters, installed into the walls or ceiling, will help make the room completely comfortable, and need be turned on only when the room is in actual use. These heaters can be recessed into the wall between the studs. Some heaters are fitted with fans to circulate the warm air.

**Wood-burning fireplace.** While a fireplace cannot be depended upon for continued everyday heating in a converted porch or garage room, it provides a cheerful supplement that may well be worth the added cost. Many people love to watch the curling colorful flames that have a tranquilizing effect. Certainly, nothing warms up a room more quickly, or with the same pleasant penetrating heat.

The chimney for a masonry fireplace is always built on its own concrete footing, which must be strong enough to support the massive, concentrated weight. The masonry fireplace itself involves critical dimensional details, the shape and proportions of the hearth, throat, and slope toward the flue all affecting the draft. Construction of a fireplace, then, should be left only to a mason who has considerable practical experience.

**Prefabricated steel fireplaces** are modern and attractive, and carry the assurance that they will function satisfactorily when properly vented. Some are free-standing, others can be mounted at a desired height on a wall. They may be used with logs, or cannel coal which burns brightly for hours and produces a steady, even heat.

Another type of prefabricated steel fireplace is designed to serve as the core of a masonry unit, providing correct design and simplifying construction details. These have air chambers that capture and circulate smoke-free heat that ordinarily would be lost up the chimney. No firebrick lining is necessary. Some models are made with curved log grates built into the bottom, and may be used without andirons. Also, there are the Heatilator prefabricated fireplaces which are open on two or more sides.

**Potbelly stoves.** Instead of a fireplace, you may be willing to settle for an old-fashioned potbelly stove. Though not really in vogue, it can be quite attractive and amusing. The stove takes up only a small space, and is easily installed with the common steel smokepipe extending through an outside wall. A more formal representation is the famed Franklin stove, at one time used all through the country. The stove burns coal as well as kindling, and provides some of the quality of the open fireplace. This stove has a swingout grill that can be used for barbeque cooking.

The floor under any free-standing stove, whether the potbelly, Franklin, or prefabricated open fireplace, should be of genuinely fireproof material that can also withstand intense heat. Suitable for this purpose are slate flagstones,

Photo shows newer thermostats made by Emerson Electric, which control both the heater and air conditioner units.

concrete flooring, quarry or ceramic tiles. Smoke pipes must be properly shielded from any flammable wall material with asbestos lining. Double-walled flue pipe is preferred, consisting of a 6-inch pipe inside an 8-inch one, with asbestos wool packed between them.

Locations of chimneys and stove vents must be considered in relation to nearby trees or the rooftop, to assure free movement of the smoke and to escape downdrafts that occur with eddying wind currents. The higher the chimney, the better the draft.

# CHAPTER ELEVEN

# FINANCING, ARCHITECTS AND CONTRACTORS

YOUR NEW recreation room can cost a substantial sum of money, anywhere from $500 if you do all the work yourself, to $5,000 and even more if you go in for all the fancy trimmings. The question then arises: how to swing the bill? How much to pay in cash and what part to borrow, and how to arrange a loan at the best terms and lowest cost, will depend on your personal circumstances and preferences. Here are some guidelines.

Paying for everything in cash is a nice and comfortable feeling, but it's not necessarily the most practical course. For some families, it is better to hold onto a major part of the savings, and pay for the home improvements in easy stages out of income. This method will incur finance charges, of course, but it's also true that you receive interest income on the savings you retain. It's a matter of how far the savings will go to balance the finance charges. That brings up the matter of your credit sources, because the charges vary greatly among different institutions.

**Depositor loans.** Savings banks in many areas will make loans to depositors up to the amount of the money on deposit, at an interest rate only 1 to 2 percent higher than the interest paid by the bank, to discourage impulsive withdrawals. Thus, if your loan is with the savings bank, you can keep your account intact and pay back the improvement loan in installments, at a nominal cost for borrowing.

Federal credit unions also make loans at very favorable rates, but this service usually is limited to members.

**Open-end mortgage.** If your mortgage is held by a bank or insurance company, it may have an "open-end" clause that provides for increasing the mortgage for home improvements to the original amount, after a large part has been paid off. This may be the best method of financing the recreation room project, with a straight low interest rate over a term of years.

Thus, if an original $12,000 mortgage has been reduced to $6,000, you may be able to borrow the necessary funds without increasing the present monthly payments very much. This will mean, though, that it will take longer than previously for you to pay off the mortgage in full and pay a little more.

But there are certain things to watch, even here. If your present mortgage has a low interest rate of 4½ or 5 percent, the bank may have the option of writing a completely new mortgage, including the total amount at the current rate, which no doubt would be higher. Thus, you would be committing yourself to pay the higher interest on the remaining $6,000 in addition to the new borrowing. This may add up to an amount that far exceeds the cost of a separate improvement loan for the smaller amount from another source.

At some institutions you might find that while the original mortgage terms would be allowed to stand as before, there may be substantial extra charges for legal, recording, and other details in revaluing the mortgage to the higher amount. Query the bank to obtain a specific list of any extra charges before taking a definite step.

**Home improvement loan.** The Federal government program for stimulating home remodeling and improvements provides a ready source of borrowing at a moderate charge. The loan is made by your local bank, and paid in monthly installments over a period of up to seven years. The difference is that the Federal government guarantees the loan. Interest charges vary somewhat at different banks, and are based on the discount system. That is, you sign a note for the full amount of the loan, but interest charge for the entire period is deducted in advance, and you receive only the remainder.

In computing the true interest rate, remember that you are making monthly payments, so that in no case is the money in your hands for the full period. Say the interest is 6 percent a year. But because you make monthly installments, the true interest is at least 12 percent considering also that the charges have been "discounted" in advance and thus you pay interest on money you did not receive—in fact, it is interest upon interest. Still, these loans are among the most favorable.

**Contractor financing.** Most contractors have some financing arrangement, either through a bank or with a factoring company. Either way, you're likely to pay much higher charges than either of the foregoing methods. A regular installment loan from a bank will carry a higher interest rate than a home improvement loan, which is guaranteed by the federal government. Financing and factoring companies often charge unconscionably high rates. A shady contractor may try to cover this up by absorbing some of the finance charges in his estimate for the work, putting the cost on a "pay so much a month" basis.

**IS AN ARCHITECT NECESSARY?** Like other professional services, the value of an architect's assistance cannot be measured by the simple yardstick of cost or need. Many home improvement projects that do not involve changes in the basic structure can, indeed, be planned and completed by the homeowner or contractor without the aid of an architect. Any homeowner with some "knowhow" can finish a basement playroom on his own. For major projects, however, architect's plans are essential. Many home-improvement contractors have a retainer arrangement with an architect, and provide the necessary services as part of the deal, included in the overall bid.

Some communities accept plans prepared and submitted by the homeowner, without further ado. Most towns, however, require that the plans be prepared and filed by an architect or civil engineer, and that they conform to the local building code and zoning ordinances. Permits must be obtained before starting the work, and the job is subject to inspection before final approval.

**Some sad experiences.** That the services of an architect are desirable for all but the most routine projects can be demonstrated by countless experiences. Many a homeowner has bemoaned his failure to obtain expert advice that would have made the renovation so much better, and in some cases prevented costly complications.

When improvements are limited to interior work that does not include tearing down partitions or making door openings in load-bearing walls, you can proceed pretty much on your own plans, provided you use materials that are approved for safety and the work conforms to the electrical and plumbing codes. Many competent contractors specialize in attic and basement finishing, do a workmanlike job based on standard materials and styling, and give excellent value for your money. If you have seen the contractor's work elsewhere and are satisfied that it meets your needs, you can safely turn over the job to him.

**What does an architect do?** There's much more to the average home improvement job than meets the eye, as is emphasized in other chapters of this book. Every room extension, of course, has walls and a roof. But so much more satisfactory will be the one that is built on adequate footings, has good surface drainage, its new walls properly tied in to the original structure with rigid insulating boards under the concrete slab and around the perimeter, vapor barrier panels on the walls, and weep holes in the siding.

Such construction details will make the room less costly to heat at a comfortable, uniform temperature; the framing members will be free of mildew and rot, no crevices will develop between the old wall and the new. In other words, the differences between amateurish run-of-the-mill work and professionally directed construction often is the difference between a good job and an unsatisfactory one.

The architect, then, is the one who is familiar with the characteristics and applications of all kinds of building materials, and specifies important details that might be overlooked even by an earnest and experienced workman. The architect eases your burden of making many difficult decisions; he assures that the plans and work conform to good building practice, that the best features of your house are retained and even enhanced, and within the scope of the new work that is undertaken, often is able to overcome longstanding flaws in the house layout, assuring the integrity of the new improvement. And for you, that adds up to carefree enjoyment of your home's facilities.

Such elaborate detailing sounds like it would skyrocket the cost. As the song goes, "it ain't necessarily so." Some of the details add only nominally to the total cost. Others may indeed represent a sizable extra charge. You can at least discuss them with the architect to evaluate the advantages relative to the cost, and decide which details or materials to retain in the plans, and which to drop. Some architects, it is true, are noted for extravagant notions, and it's up to you to call a halt when there's a tendency to put in needless and expensive frills.

**Private research.** If you have the inclination, you might be able to learn all about the building products and procedures for yourself by studying the many catalogues and specification sheets, making the rounds of display show-rooms (limited, of course, to those accessible to you) doing research on engineering reports, and getting the various and often contradictory opinions of builders. This would be a time-consuming task at best, and even so, you might overlook some good possibility that an architect would know about.

But there's even more to what you rightfully can expect from your architect. In the first place, he will know how to make the best use of your present home features, can juggle the available space for an efficient room layout, and come up with the most practical suggestions. Going further, he can make a real contribution to the final styling and appearance of your addition.

The architect also serves an important role in getting the job underway, by checking the estimates you receive and helping to select the contractor. Estimate bids may be tricky, with all sorts of reservations and hedges which the architect can recognize as they relate to his plans. He also is knowledgeable about the performance and reputations of local contractors, and can make a judicious recommendation which you may or may not follow, but which should receive due consideration.

**Architect's fees.** The American Institute of Architects issues a list of recommended fees, but architects establish their own fees in each instance according to the amount of work that will be needed, and the total cost of the project that you are planning. The easiest way to find out what the charge will be is to visit the architect at his office, discuss the project, and ask what the fee will be.

You can expect that the fee will vary from 15 to 20 percent of the total job. If you do any part of the work yourself, this will be included in the total at approximately what it would cost to have it done. When he has an idea as to the scope and quality of the work, the architect will be able to estimate the total cost and quote a fee for his services. Thus, for an attic expansion that costs $4,000 the architect's fee would be $600 to $800.

**Choosing an architect.** Your relationship with an architect is both personal and professional, and confidence is an important element. Select an architect with whom you feel comfortable in discussing your plans, and in whom you have full confidence.

You can get the names of local architects from neighbors who had recent improvement projects, from builders, or by calling the nearest office of the American Institute of Architects. It may be worth while to visit one or two at their offices to get an impression of their competence and personality, and inspect some work of the one you wish to retain. Incidentally, architects generally do not charge a fee for such a preliminary "get acquainted" discussion in their offices, but would make a charge if asked to come to your home and look over the proposed work.

If you decide to hire the architect, you will be expected to pay part of the fee as a retainer. The rest would be payable in two or three stages, when the blueprints are finished and approved, when the bids are received, and, if he has agreed to oversee the construction work, the balance when the job is completed.

Good relations go two ways. You have a right to expect that your views will be carefully noted, and are entitled to a valid explanation for any unusual departure from the expected course. On the other hand, you should cooperate fully by making up your mind as to what you expect, so that you will not have to request changes in the plans once they are completed.

**CHOOSING A CONTRACTOR.** Get a good contractor, and the project goes along smoothly, cleanly, and rapidly. The charges will be about what you would have to pay anyone else, the workers are pleasant and cooperative, some slight changes that you request in the course of the work are made without argument. The finished job is up to snuff, no loose ends and raggedy, makeshift details. It's just what you had hoped to get, but never really expected. You do your part by making the payments as agreed, and everyone's happy.

This isn't an unusual situation. Most home improvement jobs that are done by established, well-regarded firms turn out to be a happy experience for the homeowner. The masons, carpenters, electricians, and other craftsmen are experienced workers who want to get on with the job, and despite much talk to the contrary, do their work well according to current standards.

**Watch for the sharpy.** Having said this, it is necessary to raise the caution sign, because the home improvement business, which runs annually into a billion dollars or more, attracts many fast-buck operators who know all the angles and often succeed in pulling some tricky deals. They rely on the fact that the average homeowner rarely has to cope with the problem of filling out a home improvement contract, and knows very little about construction work. Some contractors do shoddy work mostly because they are not competent craftsmen and take on bargain jobs, then try to make ends meet by skimping on time and materials.

**How the gyps operate.** Many slick schemes have been perpetrated over the years by phony home improvement operators. The most common is to land the contract by quoting an exceptionally low price, then insisting on a down payment "for materials." Often, that is the last the homeowner sees of the operator, and his payment is gone. A sophisticated enlargement on this scheme is to corral a number of homeowners at one time, by offering a very attractive "group price" for obviously needed work, such as new siding, and some homeowners actually are prompted to obtain the participation of others; in effect, they become unwitting salesmen for the gyps. The deal is conditioned upon a substantial down payment by each of the homeowners, with the inevitable end that the so-called contractor collects and disappears, and the homeowners are left holding an empty bag.

**Bank loan signed.** The most vicious type of swindle is the one where the operator lands a home renovation contract and persuades the homeowner and his wife to sign bank loan notes to cover the entire cost. A new twist that has been injected is for the contractor to actually hand over a small sum of money in return, saying that it was a "rebate" on the loan! Needless to say, the contractor collects the entire proceeds from the loan, the work is never done, and the homeowner is saddled with payments for seven years.

Another painful experience encountered by more than a few homeowners is when a contractor goes bankrupt. Any down payment very likely will be lost, and if the job had been started, only the existence of a completion bond will save the homeowner from difficult and costly moves to straighten things out.

**Checking recommendations.** The oft-repeated urgings in books and magazines to deal only with "reputable" firms are not very practical. What standards can be applied to make the determination whether the firm or craftsman is "reputable" short of following back on his trail? The average homeowner is unwilling or unable to make a personal investigation even though there's much at stake.

You may be able to check by telephone one or two names supplied by the contractor as references, but unless you know these people or are convinced of their sense of responsibility, there's no assurance from that quarter. A contracting firm may do a number of jobs in the neighborhood to get some recognition, before starting a really lucrative fraud scheme.

Membership in national or local organizations is not a dependable sign of a firm's integrity, as most organizations will accept any firm that has a place of business and pays the dues. Nor is a fine office any indication—it might mean merely that the gyp has been running a lucky streak. And the Better Business Bureau, on which many people rely, may be unable to supply any conclusive information other than that the office had not received any complaints about the firm in question, which can mean not so much that its record is clear, but that it is simply a newcomer.

Several state and municipal governments have been seeking means to curb the sharp practices by some of these outfits, and in fact New York City recently enacted a law requiring the licensing of all home improvement contractors and their salesmen. A similar law was expected to pass the New York State Legislature. The purpose would be to set up ethical business standards, and provide some administrative machinery that would be able to control fly-by-night operators after investigation of complaints by homeowners.

**Obtain firm bids.** Your architect, if you have one, will supply you with a list of contractors. Even if you don't have an architect, you may find one of the local firms willing to supply the names of contractors whom they know from experience to be dependable.

Submit the blueprints to only a few selected firms for their estimates. The selection should be based on nearness of location, recommendations from an architect or neighbor, personal knowledge of the firm. A contracting firm that has a steady crew of workers also should be favored. Request that bids be submitted in writing, with specified starting and completion dates.

**Comparing the bids.** Weighing the bids is a problem in itself. There might be an astonishing disparity between the top and bottom figures. The lowest bid is not necessarily the best deal, however. The capabilities of the various firms must also be considered.

Before you make a final decision, take the time to inspect two or more jobs done by that contractor and talk with the people to learn whether the relationship was satisfactory. Then, finally, request and check bank references. But unless you have good connections, the bank may be reluctant to tell you anything more than that the firm has an account. That certainly doesn't give you any assurance about the financial condition of a firm with which you are to make a substantial commitment.

A more reliable source of this information is Dunn & Bradstreet of New York, which will furnish a current business report for a moderate fee. In the final reckoning, you should accept the bid of a contractor whose personality pleases you most, one with whom you can get along and can trust.

**Signing the contract.** No matter how likeable the contractor, and how many satisfactory jobs he's done in the neighborhood, a written contract is necessary for any major construction job. If you have a regular set of plans and specifications, drawn up by an architect, and the work is only of a limited nature such as finishing an attic or building a room extension, you could safely sign a form contract such as the standard owner-contractor agreement issued by the American Institute of Architects. But be sure to read every word typed into the contract. Balk at anything about which you have any doubt, and don't yield until you are fully satisfied as to the interpretation. Also very important, study the check list here and carefully see that all the requirements are met, in writing, not verbal assurances. A contract for an extensive home renovation job should be signed only with the advice of a lawyer.

**What to look for.** It is essential that your contract state the conditions clearly, and provide for all contingencies. This list by no means covers all possible details, nor is it in any way intended to substitute for the services of an attorney. The following are reminders of details that should be specified:

1. Whether the contrator is to supply all materials. If you are to supply any part of the materials, these should be listed, with quantities.
2. The starting and completing dates, including specified penalties for delay.
3. Whether the contractor is to obtain all necessary building and work permits.
4. That any craftsmen or subcontractors used on the job be properly licensed for their respective work.
5. Contractor to supply copies of insurance policies for public liability, workmen's compensation, and property damage coverage.
6. Completion bond, issued by an insurance company, to be obtained by the contractor at his expense.
7. Surety bond protecting homeowner against any mechanic liens.
8. Satisfactory workmanship and cleanup on completion. Any dispute to be arbitrated. Provision for escrow fund held by attorney.
9. Contractor to obtain certificate of completion or occupancy.
10. Payment schedule, as agreed, stipulating times and amounts of payment.
11. If job is financed, the institution making loan to pay proportions according to agreed schedule.
12. Changes and extra work. A time-material or other formula can be stated to cover any extras.
13. Split jobs, where you do some of the work yourself, and supply certain material. The extent of your participation should be specifically stated, and your obligations for conforming to the basic work permits and regula-

tions fully outlined, so that any defect will be placed on either you or the contractor, whoever is at fault.

**Examine policies.** For your own sake, see that your homeowner's liability policy and fire insurance cover you also while the work is in progress.

Check up on your burglary insurance, too. If the policy contains a reservation about "breaking and entering," and the house is left open during the time the job is being done, any loss of jewelry to a sneakthief may not be covered.

Once the contract is signed, the thing to do is to step aside and let the contractor proceed without annoying pressures, unless he shows definite signs of failure to live up to the contract. Then, it's a matter for lawyers, something that you've tried your best to avoid.

**BE YOUR OWN CONTRACTOR.** Suppose you plan a sizeable room extension and feel that you have enough savvy to do without a general contractor. This makes good sense if you have the leisure time, so that you will be available when needed, if you are acquainted with a large number of building trades craftsmen, if you have good sources to purchase materials at equivalent prices, are knowledgeable about going job rates, have cash available to pay for work and material, and most important, have the personal capability of getting along with the men on the job. For a retired person, it can be an interesting, creative, and productive time.

The enumeration above gives an inkling as to the extent of efforts required to coordinate a minor construction job. After the blueprints are on hand, a list of materials must be made up, the various stages of the work scheduled, commitments obtained from the different trades to come in for their roles at the proper time and get their work done in time, for the next scheduled operation to begin. It's almost like being stage manager at a Broadway production on opening night.

**Ordering materials.** Some of the materials you will need may not be stock items, or are not carried by local supply houses, so new sources must be scouted out. The materials must be ordered long beforehand, to be certain they will arrive on the job when needed; otherwise you may find yourself billed for lost working time. It's your responsibility to have everything ready to go when the men you have scheduled show up.

Provision must be made for storing the materials, sometimes for weeks. These materials, particularly building block, take up lots of room.

If you have a double garage, that might do fine, particularly for storing bags of cement, wallboard, lumber, ceiling tiles, doors, plywood, lighting fixtures, nails and the amazing number of other items that are required. In addition to protection from the weather, you will have to make sure that the materials are safe from theft. Many respectable people who would never dream of stealing anything, just seem to think that building materials are fair game to be carried off piece by piece, as builders all over the country ruefully can affirm.

As the prime contractor, then, it's your duty to get and post the necessary permits, to see that the sidewalk in front of the property is kept clear of encumbrances, and that all unusual hazards for men coming to the job are eliminated. A carpenter called in for a couple of days' work to cut some floor joists can't be expected to know that a 50-pound drum of compound was balanced precariously atop a wall by the previous gang of masons, or a hole cut in the subfloor by electricians was concealed under a piece of builder's paper. While he's covered by workmen's compensation insurance, that would not entirely clear you of a suit for injuries if you negligently failed to take reasonable precautions.

**Lining up the trades.** The really ticklish part is to line up the proper trades to follow each other up without excessive time intervals. These men are on other jobs, and must be notified just when you're ready for them. Often it means rushing out late in the evening to reach someone needed for the next day. This is a normal event in the life of a contractor, and you should at least be prepared for it. Whether things go along more or less smoothly will depend on how calm you can remain under the stress, how well you can obtain co-operation, and how well you coordinate the work.

When the job's done, though, you can expect to have great satisfaction with the result. And if you liked the pace, perhaps you will decide it's for you —and become a general contractor yourself. That's how most of the others got into the business!

# CHAPTER TWELVE

# DOING THE JOB YOURSELF

BUILDING or finishing a recreation room involves a variety of skills and abilities. Most of the work is carpentry, which includes framing walls and roof, placing floor joists or sleepers, fitting panels, furring a ceiling for tiles, fitting windows and hanging doors. Built-in furniture calls for some capability in cabinetmaking. There also will be, in some projects, much masonry work to place footings, pour a concrete slab, or build a wall with concrete blocks. Then there are tile laying, heater installation, electrical connections, insulating, a little of everything.

You can't be an expert in everything, certainly. But the fact is that much of the work can be done with just a common-sense approach, plus a little reading to learn the particular details in each situation. If you do this, you can be sure that however much the pleasure derived from your new room, and the considerable savings also, they will hardly match the satisfaction you will derive from doing a good part of the work yourself, with your own hands.

Mechanical capability is an inborn gift that is given to nearly everyone, but which is allowed to lie fallow in many people, and needs only some application to bring it to the fore. Some patience, and a careful approach to each phase of the work, will quickly give you additional assurance, increase your knowledge, and sharpen skills that you can use for many other home improvements.

**Power tools useful.** If you have any experience in handling power tools, this will be useful to speed and ease the work, making it possible for you to take on more of the project yourself. Perhaps the best first step you can take would be to get a portable saw, or a bench saw, and learn how to handle it. Power tools are not essential, but they sure help a lot. At the least, you should have a full set of hand tools, a good-quality electric drill, and an electric sabre saw which is simple and quite safe to use.

The following sections of this chapter outline some of the basic procedures for doing various parts of the work:

**ERECTING WALL STUDS.** Studs of 2-by-3 and 2-by-4 lumber are the vertical members of a wall frame for enclosing a room, building a partition wall, and also the preparatory backing for finishing an existing wall with paneling. (In the latter case, furring strips attached directly to the wall also can serve for

First step in erecting wall frame is to lay a floor plate, attached with cut nails or masonry anchors. In the basement installation shown, a plumb bob locates position of the plate.

With corner stud erected, spacer strip is nailed against the top plate for the second stud. Note that the second stud is spaced closer than 16 inches, o.c., because the wall panel covers the entire first stud facing.

When holes are to be drilled in a concrete slab or basement floor for attaching the floor plates, first drill the plates and mark the hole positions. Use a Rawl drill or carbide-tipped electric drill, being careful to stay in marked position so floor and plate holes will line up.

Floor plate spacer is nailed in place. As these spacers are short and made usually of scrap 2-by-4 ends, they may be nailed in permanently to provide additional backing for the wall panels.

Stud is checked for plumb alignment before nailing. Wall frame must be straight and true, without twists or bulges that will prevent correct alignment of the finished wall panels.

receiving the wall panels. Installation of furring strips is described later in this chapter). Use 2-by-4s for partitions, and wherever the wall stands alone. The 2-by-3s are more economical and can be used for framing basement and attic walls, but are less rigid.

**Spacing the studs.** Studs are put up 16 inches apart on centers. That is a modular measure, meaning that the spacing assures that standard 4-foot-wide wall panels will have firm backing and a nailing surface on all edges, because the center line of every third stud will be just 4 feet from the last panel joint. Also, insulation blankets are 15 inches wide, but the flanges just span the 16-inch o.c. width, to be stapled to each stud if properly spaced.

An easier way to fasten studs is provided by the new gang nails, which provide strong surface grip. After stud is erected, additional nails may be toenailed in from the sides, but the gang nails will hold the stud still for this.

Sometimes wall studs are spaced 24 inches apart o.c. (on center) for economy reasons. This is acceptable only where the studs will have additional furring strips nailed across the face of the panel installation; otherwise the panels would not have a sufficiently solid backing.

Studs must be put up plumb, straight, and uniformly spaced. Otherwise you will run into exasperating situations in fitting the wall panels, framing windows and doors, and putting in insulation batts. Like all mechanical work, the effort expended in getting the basic framework right is well repaid in easier finishing.

The studs, and all other framing lumber, should be conditioned to the room temperature for a day or two before being installed, so that they will stay true. When buying the lumber, make sure that it is kiln-dried, straight, free of twists and warps. A few tight knots are acceptable, but reject any lumber with resin streaks and large knots. Also, make sure that all the lumber is of uniform thickness and has the same mill markings, otherwise dimensional variations will add to the troubles of doing the work.

**Making stud spacer.** Locating the studs 16 inches apart o.c. sounds difficult, and certainly it is if you try to do it by measure. The studs move around when they're toenailed if not held tightly. But you can solve this neatly with the use of spacer boards which find the right location and help hold the stud steady while it's being nailed.

The spacer is cut from a selected piece of 2-by-3 or 2-by-4, whichever you are using. Mark off the 16-inch distance on the flat side, or width. Then stand a piece of 2-by-4 vertically on the inside of that line, and draw another line which will be the thickness of the 2-by-4. Saw the lumber along the inside line. That will be equal to 16 inches, less two halves of the studs. Make another of the same length, so you'll have a pair for locating at top and bottom as each stud goes up.

136

When studs are spaced 24 inches apart, horizontal members are needed, particularly for narrow knotty-pine boards. These are nailed in through the sides, with the members staggered to permit nailing at each stud.

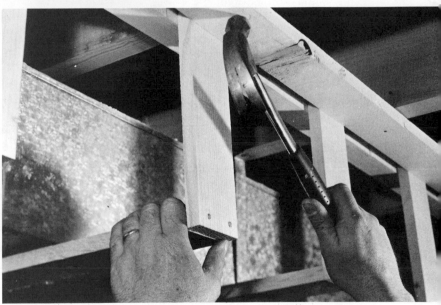

Heating ducts, soil pipes, and other installations are boxed in with lengths of ¼-inch panels. A simple wood frame is made with pieces of 1-by-3 lumber, attached to the ceiling joists.

You'll need another spacer for use where a stud starts at a corner or end wall, because the wall panel goes up over the full thickness of that stud, rather than half as in other locations. Thus, this spacer will be shorter than the others by half the thickness of a stud, which is obtained by actual measurement. These spacers should serve for the entire framing job of your room.

**Putting up the wall framing.** Start by placing a 2-by-4 on the floor as the bottom plate. It is better to attach the plate to the floor so there will be no movement of the finished wall. If the floor is of concrete, the plate can be fastened with cut nails, which are specially hardened to go into concrete, but be careful in driving them because they are brittle and can snap off. Discard any that become bent. A more secure attachment is obtained with screws into masonry anchors, for which holes must be drilled into the floor. Drilling goes very quickly with a percussion-type driver, like the Rawl rotary drill-hammer used in a regular ¼-inch electric drill.

If you're framing a wall in a converted porch, nail the top plate to a collar beam, or across from the corner posts to the end wall, making certain that it is level. In the basement, the top plate is nailed across the ceiling joists. If there is as yet no means of attaching the top plate, erect a number of the studs first, supporting them with cross braces of scrap lumber, until enough are up so the plate can be nailed on from above.

The studs are cut to uniform length, to fit snug between top and bottom plates without having to be wedged into alignment, but tightly enough so they can stand unsupported.

**Starting the studs.** The first stud starts at an end wall, preferably attached to that wall with screws. The stud is toenailed to the bottom plate, then checked with a spirit level so it is plumb before being nailed to the top plate. The stud should be flush with the front and back edges of the plates. The second stud is positioned on the bottom plate tightly against the short spacer. Toenail from the side opposite the spacer, which will help hold the stud steady. Then you can put in a nail from the other side. Do the same at the top, starting the nail first, then holding the spacer with one hand while you drive the nail home. For the next studs, use the regular size spacer. After each stud is up, check it with the spirit level, and correct any deviations from the plumb. Also, when half a dozen or so studs are up, check their alignment with a long straight board. Correct the position of any studs which are out of line.

This is fundamentally the process of framing a wall. But there are some additions, which include openings for radiators, recessed built-ins, and windows and doors. Wherever these are needed, the studs are cut around headers, which are horizontal members across the openings. Another detail is that floor plates are omitted at locations of doorways.

In a room that is not precisely of modular dimensions, you will find that the end of each wall leaves a space beyond the last stud that is less than the 16-inch distance. If the space is only a few inches, don't make the mistake of "stretching" the last stud. It won't work, as the panels require the regular spacing. The extra gap may need another stud, if it is wide enough, otherwise nail a strip of furring to the edge of the corner studs to provide a nailing face for the panels into the corner.

**Attic walls.** About the only variation from the above in framing a wall is in the attic, where the knee walls are attached directly to the roof rafters. Find the location where the rafters clear the attic floor by at least 4 feet, and chalk a line.

Fasten a plate of 1-by-4 lumber to the joists or wood floor behind the chalked line. Cut the 2-by-4's with an angle at one end matching the slope of the rafters, and to a length that will fit between the floor plate and under the roof boards. Nail the stud to the rafter, and toenail to the floor plate. Cut lengths of either 1-inch stock or 2-by-4 to fit between the rafters, each piece cut and fit individually because of some variation in the distance. These pieces are nailed up between the knee wall studs so that the top edge of these cross-pieces is at the angle where the rafter crosses the upright studs.

Enclose each stud-rafter section in this way. Then attach similar pieces between the rafters just above the first crosspieces. These are put in to provide nailing faces for the panels which will go on the knee walls and on the sloped part of the ceiling. A word of caution: when driving nails into roof rafters back up the rafter with the head of a sledge to prevent movement of the drafter and possible shifting of roof shingles.

**Openings for windows.** The end wall studs similarly are based on a floor plate, but extended at varying heights according to the slope of the end rafter, limited by the height of the ceiling beam which will enclose the remaining roof section near the peak. There usually are windows at these end walls, but if not, provision should be made for installing the windows.

Also see that where the knee and end walls meet, the corners are closed in with a stud or 1-inch lumber nailed to the end studs, so the panel edges can be nailed. The window dimensions should be obtained beforehand. The frame allows at least 1 inch extra clearance at the width and height. The frame is made by fitting a horizontal 2-by-4 member between studs at the desired height above the floor, driving the nails through the sides of the studs into the end of the horizontal 2-by-4. Then put in the header across the top of the frame, securely nailed through the side studs.

**CEILING BEAMS.** Erection of attic ceiling collar beams is described in Chapter 5. The ceiling in a converted porch that has a pitched roof may remain as it is, the underside of the rafters finished with tongue-and-groove knotty pine boards or other paneling over insulation. If a level ceiling is desired, however, ceiling joists of 2-by-6 lumber may be put in under the present roof. A 2-by-4 cleat is attached to the rear wall of the room with heavy fasteners to hold the joists. This support must be well secured with bolts into masonry anchors. The front end of the beams is supported on the top wall plate. If the plate is not accessible, nail up a 2-by-4 supporting corbel along the front, 2 inches lower than the rear cleat, and attached to the inside face of the top wall plate. The joists are cut to length to span the room, front to back, and one end of each joist is cut at a sharp angle matching that of the sloped roof rafter against which it must fit when supported on the front corbel. The rear corner is notched to a 2-inch depth so it will lock into the end corbel and come down level with the front end which rests on the wall plate. These joists are spaced 16 inches apart o.c., and nailed to their supporting members. In a roof with a level ceiling below, the insulation is fitted between the ceiling joists, leaving the upper section as an open air space which must be vented on both sides.

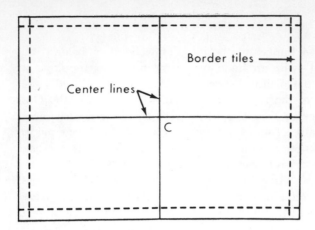

Diagrams show layout for planning both ceiling and floor tile installations. The objectives are two-fold: to assure that the tiles will run parallel to the walls, and that the border tiles will be of uniform width. Make sure lines are at right angles.

Room is measured across at both ends to find center, then the center line is moved over if necessary so that the rows of tiles will end with equal width, rather than a very narrow strip. Measurements are taken of both width and length of the room. At the adjusted center line, tiles are started in all directions.

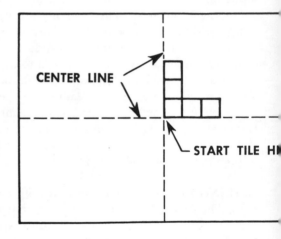

**FURRING FOR WALL PANELS.** Inexpensive 1-by-3 furring strips may be fastened directly to masonry walls, thus eliminating the need for an extensive framing with 2-by-4 studs. Furring has the twin purposes of providing a nailing surface for wall panels and also allowing an air space back of the panels. In addition to costing far less than the heavy 2-by-4 lumber, it takes up smaller space, saving a few inches at each side of the room, which sometimes may be important.

The strips are fastened to the wall with cut nails, or a special device like Shure-Set, made by the Ramset division of Olin Matheison Company and priced at just a couple of dollars. The kit consists of a cylindrical tool with a metal piston at the center. A special fastener is inserted into the bottom. Several sharp blows on the steel piston will drive the sharply pointed fastener pin through the wood strip and into any masonry wall. The pin is driven about ½

Furring strips on ceiling must be properly spaced so edges of tiles will meet at center of the strip, as shown in this photograph. A strip is also placed along all the end walls.

An advanced method of ceiling tile installation without furring strips uses a "Clip-Strip" system. Metal strips, made by Gold Bond, are nailed to ceiling joists, receive tile tongues.

to 1 inch in concrete, ¾ to 1¼ inches in concrete blocks and fresh concrete. The fasteners are available in an assortment of lengths, from ¾ to 3 inches, and some have threaded studs for attaching brackets and other items to walls.

**Using concrete fastener.** The furring then is merely held in place at one end and a fastener driven into the wall to hold it. Now there's one problem— the wall never is straight across. If the pins were driven in at intervals they would make the furring conform to the wall shape, and the surface paneling also would be wavy. To avoid this, place wood shims of the necessary thickness wherever the wall recesses out of line. The pins can be placed at any locations, but use enough so the furring is securely fastened. And check the installed furring with a straightedge board for alignment.

Furring strips are put up horizontally on a wall, except at the ends where vertical strips also are needed. You can decide for yourself how far apart to space the strips, but 16 inches would be the maximum; otherwise the wall panel edges may be insufficiently supported. Before starting, check the wall with a plumb bob, as it may be out of alignment. Usually the lower part extends out farther than the top, and in that case, start the furring at the bottom, working upwards and shimming out as you go to end up with a plumb wall.

**Furring for ceiling tiles.** Use 1-by-3 strips for nailing across the ceiling joists. Start against the end walls, nailing the first strips close to those walls. Before the rest go up, you want to see how the ceiling tiles will add up in the space. You don't want to have full-sized tiles along one or two walls, then wind up with narrow strips against the other ends. Better measure out the room, and figure the placement so that anything less than a full tile is divided equally at both walls. Then shift the center a few inches either way to achieve this and put up the first furring strip at that new "center" line. See to it, too, that the furring does not drift off to one side so the tile lines will be distorted. Measure the walls at both ends and equalize the center furring, then make sure all the others go up parallel to each other.

From there, space out the rest of the furring according to the size tiles you will use, either 12 or 16 inches o.c., though some tiles, like U.S. Gypsum Acoustone use a spline clip installation and can be put on strips 48 inches apart. As the furring strips go up, watch to see that they are correctly spaced all along; otherwise the tile tongues won't fall in place. Also, see that the strips are uniformly level, shimming where the joist is too high, and notching a bit if the joist is too low.

**PUTTING UP CEILING TILES.** For tongue-and-groove tiles, you will need a stapling gun that can shoot staples with 5/16-inch or longer legs, so they will fasten the tile flanges to the furring. Other installation systems include U.S. Gypsum's Z-spline fasteners, which are held up with spline clips, nailed to the furring or even directly to the ceiling joists.

Acoustical tiles, made of mineral fibers, can be cut on a circular saw, with a hand saw, or a razor-sharp knife. A number of the tiles will have to be cut to fit along the walls.

Tiles come in various sizes, mostly 12 by 12 and 12 by 24 inches. There are also 16- and 24-inch squares.

Before you start installing the tiles, bisect the room with chalked lines across the ceiling, meeting at true right angles at the center. The lines will serve as your guide to keep the tile courses straight in relation to the room walls. You won't want to climb down the ladder and find that the tiles trail off towards one wall.

**Locating the tiles.** When you've found the approximate width for the end wall tiles, cut a few tiles to that size and put up the first tile into a corner. The part you cut has the tongues, leaving the flanged sides for stapling. Put two

Photo shows how cove molding supports border tiles and covers nails driven into edge of tiles. Installation may start at a corner instead of room center, once the border tile size is determined.

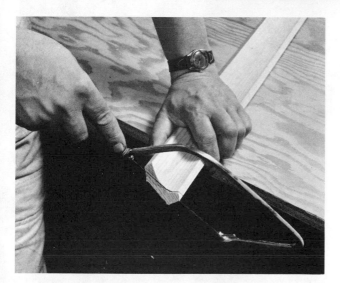

Crown molding is tricky, as it can't be mitered in the ordinary way, but rather is coped to make the joint. First, place molding in miter box in same position it will go on wall, with back against the rear fence. Cut at 90-degree angle. Then remove stock from the back with a coping saw, as shown.

Sample pieces show how the coped molding pieces should fit together in mitered joint at corner. This is because the second molding strip has been carved to the shape of the first, so the faces join tightly.

Floor finishing has been greatly simplified by the new adhesives that are simply brushed on like paint. Installation starts at the center lines of the room, the tiles laid toward the walls. Chalk lines are snapped after adjusting for even width of tiles along end walls.

Tiles are laid on center lines, then butted together as they are joined in the continuing installation. Once the work is started, the floor goes very quickly.

Make sure that each tile is correctly seated before starting the next. The tiles should butt uniformly against the adjacent tiles on two sides.

An easy way to find the correct width of end tiles that will go against the walls. Place a full tile exactly above the last course, then place another tile on top, pushed against the wall, and score the bottom tile. When cut, the lower tile will be correct width to fit the space.

Tile snaps off along the scored line. For softer vinyl tiles, cut with tinsnips or heavy scissors.

Tile is smoothed into place. After installation, roll the tiles so they are flattened down and bonded by the adhesive.

staples into each flange. Now proceed from there, working in both directions from the corner, and also toward the center of the room, watching to see that the courses are straight. It may be that some of the border tiles going against one wall must be cut to slightly different widths because of variations in the wall.

Joining the tongue-and-groove tiles must be done gently, making sure that each tile is truly centered with the next before it is stapled. Avoid forcing the tiles tightly together, as this will cause bulging of the surface around the groove, and also affect the alignment. Rather, merely push each new tile just enough so its tongues are firmly seated.

The final course of tiles will not have a nailing flange, because they are cut to fit snug against the wall. Instead, they are nailed through the surface of the tile to the furring strip parallel to the wall. Counterset the nailheads, which will be covered later with crown molding trim.

**SUSPENDED PANEL CEILING.** A more modern method of ceiling installation without furring strips is the Armstrong suspended ceiling system. The ceiling consists of 2-by-4-foot acoustical ceiling panels supported by a simple metal framework which is hung by wires from the existing ceiling joists or rafters. In basements, the ceiling can be hung low enough to clear the pipes and ducts,

Suspended ceiling installation starts by finding the desired level, at any distance below the ceiling joists. Plan the installation so that new ceiling covers all ducts, pipes, and other room obstructions.

Locate position of first ceiling runner after finding width of border tiles, as in conventional tile installation. Turn a screw eye into the ceiling joist in line with the runner.

Install the first metal runner by fastening to bent wire. Attach a hanger wire every 4 feet for adequate support. Continue this procedure across the room until all main runners are installed.

The 4-foot cross Tees are placed between main runners at 24-inch intervals. Insert the end tab of a cross Tee into the runner slot and push in to lock it in place.

With supports all in place, ceiling tiles now can be laid into the grid. Tilt the panel slightly upwards, slide through the opening, and rest the panel on the grid flanges. In place of the regular panel, translucent plastic may be used for lighting effects with fluorescent lamps installed between the joists.

while in attics it can be raised or lowered from the collar beams to span the precise width of the room regardless of the pitch of the roof.

Installation starts by nailing a molding to the walls around the room at the selected ceiling height, to support the suspension structure. Then attach wires to the joists or rafters at 4-foot intervals. The main runners of the metal framework are attached to these wires, and cross-tees snapped into place between these runners, thus forming a grid for the new ceiling.

The ceiling panels are then simply laid into the framework to complete the installation. The panels can be lifted out whenever access to the area above is desired. These ceiling panels are quite large, 2-by-2 and 2-by-4-feet in size.

Recessed lighting is easily installed with the suspended ceiling. Translucent plastic panels can be incorporated into the framework beneath a fluorescent fixture mounted above, or the entire ceiling can be of such panels to give a totally luminous effect. You can control the lights with a dimmer switch, or have a gang switch to select the degree of lighting desired.

Typical framing for large picture windows. Frames are put in
before glazing, temporarily held with cross braces.

Completed sliding windows with sills and trim. Modern wood
windows are supplied with factory weatherstripping, which is a
decided saving on work on the site.

148

**FRAMING DOORS AND WINDOWS.** For door openings in the wall, allow a space of 5½ inches plus the width of the door between the last studs at each side of the opening. If there is a framing plate on the floor across the opening, saw the plate to remove the section, cutting close to the side face of the end studs. Cut a 2-by-4 header long enough to reach between the end studs. Now a second stud is added on each side, to double up for the greater strength. These studs are cut to the height of the door, plus an extra 2½ inches. The studs fit against the sawed floor plate, and are nailed to the end studs. The header goes across the top of these double studs, and is nailed both to them and to the end studs. A vertical cripple stud is fitted and nailed at the center of the header, reaching to the ceiling plate.

The door opening is finished with jambs across the top and on the sides, of 1-inch stock (actually about ¾-inch thickness). Before nailing the jambs, place flat spacer shims between them and the studs, and check that the jambs are plumb before driving the nails home. If necessary, leave several of the shims in place to true up the jamb.

The nails are located at about the center line on the jamb, where they will be covered with the final door-stop strip. Put the door into the opening to see that it fits squarely, then nail up the trim molding around the door frame, to cover the shims. The door trim goes on before the walls are finished, as the panels will be fitted closely against the inside edges of the trim.

**HANGING THE DOOR.** Planing the door to fit perfectly into the frame, and the rest of the work of mortising hinges and lock, will be done much more easily and correctly if you make a simple floor jack to hold the door steady while you work on it. The jack consists of two pieces of 2-by-4, nailed to a strip of 1-inch wood with a separation between the blocks just large enough for the thickness of the door to fit between them. The bottom strip is raised above the floor on two pieces of scrap 1-inch lumber, set at right angles to the blocks to keep the jack steady.

Simple door jack, made of scrap lumber, supports doors while they are planed and mortised. Center clearance is just large enough to admit entry of the door.

With the door in the wall opening, raised by a wood strip the thickness of the threshold you will use, mark the spots where the door is too tight against the jamb. Set the door into the floor jack and plane where necessary. Avoid taking off long strips of wood along one side, as that would make the door look crooked when hung. If necessary, adjust the framing jambs. But see that the door has just enough clearance at the side and top to swing out. With the door in place, locate the door stop, and also mark the door and side jamb for the hinges.

Mortising is done with a sharp chisel. First drive straight down into the wood to outline the mortise cut along the sides of the hinge leaf, then remove the stock in a number of chisel cuts about ⅜-inch apart. Stay within the marked lines, and don't cut too deeply before checking to see how the hinge leaf fits. Clean out the stock so the mortise is of uniform depth and perfectly smooth.

The leaf should fit quite tightly in the mortise, with no movement in any direction, and flush with the door surface. Make pilot holes with a drill or a punch for the hinge screws, keeping these holes toward the back to pull the leaf in tighter in the mortise when the screws are tightened. Make the mortises in the jamb the same way, checking to see that the half hinge leaves line up with those on the door edge. Attach each side of the leaf separately, then hang the door by tapping in the hinge pins. If the door binds, it may need a bit of further planing, or it can be freed up by inserting paper shims behind the hinge leaves on the jamb to square up the door.

For installing the lock, use the template provided by the manufacturer as a guide for drilling the required holes. With the lock in position, you can mark the location for the latch plate, which is mortised into the jamb after a sufficient depth has been drilled or chiseled out to provide clearance for the spring latch.

**OPENING A DOORWAY IN A WALL.** Locate the new door a few inches on one side from an existing stud, and where you are sure there is no heating or plumbing pipe in the wall. Interior doors are standard 30-inch width, and that means you will have to cut away two existing studs to clear the opening. Allow 2 inches more width, and 3 inches more height (including the threshold) than the door size.

Mark the opening directly on the wall, using a plumb bob to align the sides, and a level to square off the top line.

Nail straight boards to the wall on the outside of these lines as guides for cutting the plaster and to protect the rest of the wall from unnecessary damage. If the wall is of wallboard or gypsum boards, clean cuts can be made by deeply scoring the surface with a wall knife which uses razor blades as the cutting edge, running the blade against the wood guide strips. When the lines are deeply scored, you can break several holes in the wall with a hammer in order to snap the wall panels off at the scored lines.

**Cutting into plaster.** If the wall is of wet plaster on rock lath, the plaster can be cut with a wood chisel, but that will be quite messy and difficult. An easier way is to use a carborundum blade in a portable saw, set to make a very shallow cut with each pass. In using the saw, relocate the guide strips so the saw shoe will ride against them with the blade on the marked lines.

Another way to cut the plaster is to make a few small holes inside the marked lines and use a keyhole saw with a special hardened blade. Several blades will be worn through before the job is finished.

**Reinforce the opening.** With the wall opening completed, a header and two studs are put in, securely joined to form the frame for the door. First cut a 2-by-4 header long enough to fit between the present studs inside the wall. Cut two vertical studs, the length equal to the 6-foot, 8-inch height of the door plus the thickness of the threshold, and the 1-inch top jamb. Maneuver the header into the wall, resting one end on top of a stud. Nail them securely together. Now raise this stud so it goes against the present stud at one side of the wall opening, and nail the new stud to it. The header is supported at the free end by inserting the second stud at the other side of the opening. This stud is fastened by toenailing to the floor plate, to the header, and with a few nails through the wall close to the opening where the nailheads will be covered with the wide door case molding.

The door is fitted and hung as described previously in this chapter. Any damage to the wall that would be visible is patched with plaster before the door trim is nailed on.

**GYPSUM WALL PANELING.** One of the most widely used wall paneling materials is gypsum boards, of which the names Sheetrock and Gold Bond are familiar to everyone. In addition to their economy, the gypsum panels are among the lowest-cost wall materials you can use, they have an excellent fire-resistance rating, provide a perfectly smooth surface for painting, wallpapering, or even laminating Formica. When properly installed on a suitable wood frame, the panels are permanent and troublefree.

Gypsum wallboard is cut with razor blade or sharp wall knife by scoring along a clamped guide strip, then snapping the panel end downward so it snaps. Finally, cut through paper at back.

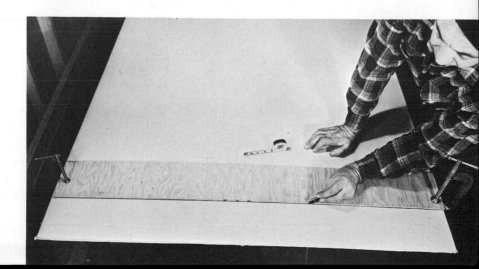

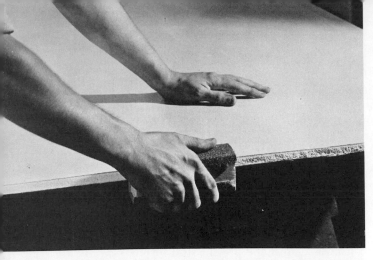

If panel edge is uneven, with slight bumps that will prevent fitting into the opening, use a sanding block to smooth them down, otherwise the panel will crack if forced into smaller space.

Gypsum panels are nailed to wall frame as specified in the text, nails no closer than ⅜ inch from the edge. Panel joints may be finished with special tape and joint compound.

Panels come in 4-foot widths, lengths from 6 to 12 feet. The most common thicknesses used for home installation are ⅜ and ½ inch. These panels are quite heavy and have to be handled with care to avoid crushing the corners before the panels are put up. The panels may be either glued to the wall frame with a bead adhesive, or nailed with special ringed drywall nails. For more rigidity, soundproofing and fireproofing, double panels on the walls are recommended, though the single panels will be quite adequate in basement and attic rooms, and for walls in room extensions, like the porch and garage where there is insulation on the outside wall.

Gypsum panels come in many types. Some have regular square edges for butting the panels together; others have tapered edges for sealing the panel joints with a special perforated tape and a plaster coating.

These wall panels are suitable for installation in any location except where they would be subject to excessive moisture or occasional wetting.

**Cutting the panels.** Gypsum panels are easy to cut, using a razor knife against a wood guide strip. The panel is placed over sawhorses, the waste end overhanging the front. The guide strip is held or clamped in place, and the knife blade run against the guide to score the panel deeply. Then the end is snapped down, breaking along the scored line. With the knife, slice the other side of the paper backing, and the cut is completed.

A prime requirement for good gypsum board installation is that the wall studs be straight and uniformly in alignment, as otherwise the panels will be pulled in out of line by the nails, and might eventually spring away. With a carefully constructed frame, installation of the panels is quite simple.

Many accessories are available for all installation conditions, including inside and outside corner trim, reinforcing strips, joint channels, jointing tape, and nails.

For a recreation room with average ceiling height, installation is easiest when the panels are installed horizontally, one 4-foot-wide panel above the other. The lower panel rests on a baseboard of the same thickness which is attached to the floor plate. The adhesive bead is spread over the stud faces and headers that are to be covered, the panels then set in place and nailed to the studs. The nails are driven so the heads are counterset just enough to dimple, so that the nailheads can be covered with compound.

A special nailing procedure should be followed when putting up gypsum panels to assure good results. Always hold the board tightly in contact with the wall as the nail is being driven, so that the nail holds the panel where it is rather than drawing it back toward the wall, with subsequent damage to the plaster core in this process. Start nailing at the center, working toward the edges. Place nails in vertical lines along the studs, spaced no more than 8 inches apart. At the ends of each side, put in nails not closer than ⅜ inch from the edge.

In a double-nailing system, the first nails are spaced 12 inches apart, starting from center and working outwards in both directions, with a row of edge nails 8 inches apart. Then return and put in a second course of nails, 2 to 2½ inches above the first, but not along the edges, where the single nails remain.

**Double panel installation.** Double layers of Sheetrock for two-ply wall thickness are recommended both for solidity and insulation value. The second surface panels are put up vertically over the horizontal ones, using both adhesive and nails. Only a small number of nails need be placed to hold the panels until the adhesive forms a bond. Installation of the panels without nails requires

When knotty pine boards are used for wall finishing, they should be finished before being nailed up. A coating with white paint thinly mixed with Firzite will give that popular light-tone effect. Prefinishing is easier than after the panels are on the wall.

Knotty pine panels are nailed to the frame with finishing nails driven through the tongues, so that no nailheads will be on the panel surface. Nails are driven also through top and bottom ends where they will be covered by moldings.

propping the panels with temporary supports to provide adequate pressure for the adhesive.

**Finishing the wallboard.** Gypsum paneling may be painted or covered with wallpaper. If the panel joints have not been taped, an application of plain muslin will cover the joints sufficiently so that they do not show through the wallpaper. Molding strips, applied as battens or to form squares on the wall, can also serve to cover the joint openings.

There are things you will quickly learn about gypsum board, and equally about plaster, as you proceed with the installation. One is that there's absolutely no "give" or resiliency to the plaster. If you have to fit a piece of the gypsum wallboard into a certain place, make sure to cut it exactly to size, or even somewhat smaller. If the panel is just a tiny bit too long, don't force it into position, as the panel will break or at least the ends will crack off.

Another thing is to watch the corners of the panel as you work with it and move it around. The plaster is really tough on the wall, and as mentioned previously, can't be compressed to the slightest degree, but let the panel strike the floor or any surface, and the corner will crumple. This isn't too serious, as the end can be trimmed or the corner cut off neatly so the small space can be patched with plaster after the panel is nailed up.

Touching up nailheads and any surface damage with plaster of paris will provide a smooth and neat surface for painting and papering.

One type of Sheetrock comes prefinished with a paper coating in cherry, ranch pine, or sablewood colors and wood graining from photographic reproductions. Colored nails are used for inconspicuous nailing.

**PLYWOOD AND MARLITE WALL PANELS.** Installation of both plywood and plastic-coated wall paneling follows the same basic procedure, though there are some differences in the nailing, the accessories, and the final trimming.

As in all wall finishing, a strong frame of studs, spaced 16 inches o.c. is required, or furring on a solid wall to provide air space behind the panels. Where panels are installed in locations below grade, a vapor barrier between the wall and the panels is necessary to prevent trapped moist air and condensate.

Before starting the installation, remove the panels from their cartons and wrappers, separate them in the room for conditioning of at least 48 hours so they will stabilize to the existing humidity and temperature.

The panels may be installed vertically flush with the floor, but in that case the floor should be checked to see that it is level all around the walls. Do this by snapping a chalk line a few inches above the floor, and measuring to find the highest point. An alternative is to permanently nail a level supporting base a few inches high, of ¼-inch stock, on which the panels rest for installation. This base will be covered later with the finish base and shoe molding.

**Aligning the panels.** The first panel against a corner wall must be put up absolutely plumb. Place the panel on the baseboard and slide it into the corner. Use a spirit level to make certain that the panel edge is plumb. At the corner, the panel may touch the end wall at only one or two points, usually the lower part of the edge. Run a scriber or wing divider, spread about 2 inches, along the wall to mark the wall's contours along the plywood. With a sharp plane, remove the excess plywood as marked, and try the fitting again. Several repeated markings and planings will be necessary to get the panel flush into the corner, plumb on both the long panel edge and the face. Before fastening the panel, test the fit by placing a second panel against it on the base to see that the edges butt tightly together the full length.

**Attaching the panels.** Panel adhesive, available from both U.S. Plywood Company and the Marlite Company, comes in a cartridge that is used in a typical calking gun. Snip the end of the cartridge snout and apply beads of adhesive about ⅛-inch thick on the stud face or furring. Marlite recommends a continuous ribbon of adhesive along all the surfaces, while U.S. Plywood suggests intermittent strips of adhesive about 4 inches long. Do one panel at a time.

Apply the panel immediately. Position the panel, then press firmly against the adhesive. Hammer three or four finishing nails part way in along the top edge to hold the panel in correct position, then pull out the bottom from the wall a few inches, placing a spacer block behind to hold the panel away from the wall until the adhesive dries.

After about 10 minutes, remove the block, ease the panel into final position, then tap the panel along the studs by hammering on a wood block to assure good contact. Hammer in the top finishing nails, countersinking the heads so the holes can be covered with matching Putty Stik filler. The nail-heads won't be visible at the ceiling level, and in any event will be covered with the crown or cove molding.

The next panels should need no edge trimming for alignment, as they will square up with the first panel on that wall when edges are butted together.

Continue in the same manner to fit the remaining panels around the room. With the 4-foot coverage of each panel, and the fast adhesive method of installation without nailing, the entire installation will go quickly.

**Prepare each panel first.** Be sure to make all necessary cuts in each panel, before installation, for electric receptacles and switches, around doors and windows, air conditioner, heater, and other room equipment. Where there are low-voltage wires that will be needed for connections later, for the telephone, intercom, and thermostat, drill the panel at the correct position and draw the wires through the hole before installation.

Prefinished hardwood trim, or aluminum moldings with hardwood veneer facings to match the panels, are used to give the room a professionally designed appearance. Shapes include inside and outside corners, divider strips to cover panel joints, cap channel, and molded plywood ceiling cove. Finish moldings of matching solid hardwood are available for ceiling crown, door casing, door stop, window stool, base, and shoe.

Prefinished Weldwood and similar plywood, and Marlite and Masonite Panelcote paneling, need no staining or painting after installation. The walls go up, and the room is finished, looking exactly as you expected from the original samples from which you made your selection. Therefore, be careful when handling and sawing the panels to avoid marring the fine surface finish.

**MASONRY WORK.** Any recreation room project that involves building an addition to your house brings you into the question of concrete work. Whether or not you can do this yourself will depend more on the amount of leisure time you have and the willingness to tackle a new kind of work, than any previous experience, because concrete is a handyman's material.

The actual labor is not as arduous as it appears, or once was, mostly because of pre-mixed concrete, or small electric mixers that can be rented by the day. The amount of excavating is small, and won't take too long, as the most you would have to do is dig a trench for a footing. That is, of course, if you don't insist on excavating for a full basement area under the new room.

A footing, and perhaps a low wall of concrete blocks, will be necessary if your room will be built on a concrete slab. Also, if you are converting a grade-level porch and want to make it larger than it is now, the present porch floor will be extended with a concrete slab.

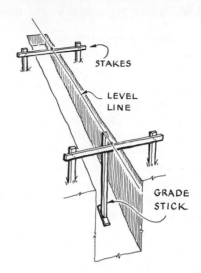

STAKES

LEVEL
LINE

GRADE
STICK

When putting in a footing, find the level line by drawing a taut string along the top between stakes. Tie one end of the string to an end stake, holds the other with windings around the other end stake. Use a line level and raise or lower the loose end string as needed, then tie it in place. A grade stick will show when the trench bottom is of uniform depth.

A room above grade level can be built with masonry piers or lally columns supporting the floor joists. These columns must have adequate concrete footings. The area under the room may be left open or enclosed with a curtain wall for a crawl space.

**Squaring the base.** One of the most important steps in concrete work is to lay out the walls or position of the column supports so they are square with the house. Don't depend on doing this by sighting or measurements. But there is a simple and dependable way that will assure a correct guide for you to proceed.

When you've determined the length and width of the new construction, put up 1-by-4-inch batter boards at each far corner, assuming there will be two extended corners away from the house. These batter boards may be of rough scrap lumber, but solid. Drive three 2-by-2-inch stakes into the ground at each corner, outside your tentative corner line. One stake is diagonally away from the corner, the others about 3 feet from that corner post, on each side. Thus each corner has a sort of short right-angle fence.

The problem is to find the true right angles for your footing corners. Tie a taut string across the far length of the designated space, between two boards. Also tie strings from the house wall, at the point where the new wall is to meet it, stretched taut to the boards at the far end.

Now you will use an ancient bit of geometry to square those lines precisely. Cut three pieces of wood, to 3-, 4-, and 5-foot lengths, and join them into a triangle with the outer corners meeting precisely, and nail the corners together. The angle formed by the intersection of the two shorter pieces will be a right angle. Use this to square the corners, shifting the strings as necessary to conform to the wood triangle. Test the correctness by stretching lines diagonally across from one corner to the other; both lines should be precisely the same length.

**Digging the footings.** The excavation for the footings must go down to the frostline, and 6 inches deeper. This is between 3 and 4 feet in most northern localities. The rule about footings is that they should be twice the thickness of the masonry wall, and have a depth equal to the thickness of the wall. Thus, if the curtain or foundation will be of 8-inch concrete block, the footing will be 16 inches wide, and extend in the trench at least 8 inches. Use a good steel tape for measuring, not a folding rule.

The bottom of the excavation should be of firm soil, and cleared to a uniform depth. Set up wood forms, of 1-by-8 or 2-by-8 boards, securely staked on the outside, with temporary bridging across the top of the forms. The height of the form will show the depth of the footing.

**Figuring the concrete.** The amount of concrete needed should be computed, so you have enough to do each part of the work at one time. The footing need not be fully cured before you proceed to lay in the needed courses of concrete blocks for the foundation wall, or curbing for the slab floor.

One big drawback in ordering ready-mix is the difficulty of moving the concrete to the backyard diggings. The mixer truck could not be driven into the back, even if there were access, without causing considerable damage to driveway or shrubbery. And transporting the concrete in a wheelbarrow is not practical as you pay for excessive standby time.

If a fair amount of concrete will be needed, it will be best to rent a ¼-yard-capacity electric mixer for a day or two.

To make approximately a ¼-yard of concrete, mix 2 cubic feet of cement (one bag holds exactly 1 cubic foot), 3 cubic feet of sand and 5 cubic feet of crushed stone together. Add sufficient water to bring the mixture to the consistence of mud.

The footing form is filled flush with the top of the wood forms, which should be level. After the concrete has set, remove all the stakes, wood bridging, and the form boards. Make sure to clear out all pieces of wood before backfilling.

For laying in the concrete wall blocks, stretch guide strings across, using a line level and adjusting the string to proper height. Watch that the blocks are placed plumb, checking the wall with a plumb bob suspended from a horizontal cross arm attached to a post above the wall.

**Pouring the slab.** Prepare the soil by excavating down to firm soil. Put down an 8-inch layer of crushed stone, then cover with a vapor shield of plastic membrane, or heavy roofing paper overlapped 3 inches along the edges, and turned up 6 inches along the walls.

Also, line the inside perimeter of the wall with rigid insulating blocks, so that the concrete slab is separated from the wall. Place a capillary vapor shield between the foundation and the start of the masonry wallblocks. At this point, also, there should be a metal termite shield, below the starting level of the outside siding.

The surface of a concrete slab is finished smooth with the use of a striking board and trowel, to work the pebbles down into the concrete.

# INDEX